Advance Praise

"The world is ready for this book."
—Robert Edson Swain, Green Architect

"Living Green *provides a brilliant and user-friendly guide to healthy and conscious living."*
—Marci Zaroff, Founder/President—Under the Canopy

"Living Green *is perhaps the most meaningful 'how to' guide for creating wellness I have ever read. The industry of wellness is so full of rhetoric that the consumer is understandably left bewildered. In this book, one is not introduced to a fad, but rather an artistically communicated view of intelligent existence. The brilliance of* Living Green *is its integration. It addresses what to put in your body and on your body. How to change your home and your world. Greg Horn's obvious genius will change your life. Read and act on this book."*
— Patrick Gentempo, Jr., D.C., CEO, Creating Wellness Alliance

"I read this book and was possessed. As someone both personally and professionally dedicated to the outdoor lifestyle, I see the compelling need to do things differently. Nature depends on it, and the situation is critical. Greg's book convinced me that I could make a difference, which I didn't believe before I read it. At last I knew exactly what I could do to participate in this whole new way of life."
—Michelle Barnes, Outdoor Products Association

"Living Green *is a must-read for anyone seeking practical ways to start changing the world now. Real life experiences and practical tips make this a road map for personal action. This book helps you get past the worry and do something green."*
—Anthony Zolezzi, Chairman of The Organic Center,
Co-Author of *Chemical Free Kids* (Kensington, 2003)
and CEO of Natural Pet Nutrition

A Message from Paul Zane Pilzer, Author of The Wellness Revolution

We were riding the ski lift when Greg first told me about this book. Right away, I knew it was going to be great. For years, Greg has been my personal nutrition coach, giving me insight into what works and what doesn't work as we have pedaled, hiked and skied the mountain trails and slopes around Park City.

Over the years I've introduced Greg to dozens of my friends, and they all say the same thing: His advice works, and it's easy to see why.

I first met Greg when he was CEO of GNC, where he sat in the catbird seat over the emerging wellness revolution. His new work at Garden of Life has given him a broad view of the organic movement and its health and environmental implications from soil to shelf. The passion and energy he brings to his own active outdoor lifestyle spills over into his personal commitment to health and sustaining our environment.

Greg's unique access to leading thinkers, nutrition expertise, and scientific approaches—plus his CEO's bias towards action—lets him bring it all together so we can take action too.

And there is compelling reason to take action. Greg knows that people want to do something about their wellness, but don't know where to start. This book inspires action without being heavy-handed or depressing. It offers practical tips you can act on to make a difference.

Finally, someone has made it easy to be green.

Living Green:
A Practical Guide for
Simple Sustainability

by Greg Horn

Freedom
Press

Cover design by Foerstel Design
Book design by Bonnie Lambert

ISBN 1-893910-47-4

First printing
Printed in the United States

Published by Freedom Press
1861 North Topanga Canyon Boulevard
Topanga, CA 90290

To our children, and theirs...

FOREWORD

VERY FEW PEOPLE get a second chance at life. My near-fatal battle with an "incurable" disease was won by following age-old dietary and lifestyle principles including the consumption of organic, living and sustainably produced foods. My healthy diet and lifestyle gave me a second chance, and put me on a path of wellness that continues today.

We live in a world where the population is multiplying, natural resources are becoming scarce and the evidence of our damage to the planet is mounting. We are surrounded by riches, yet destroying ourselves with massive over-consumption of our precious natural resources. We know this is a global problem, and we want to do our part to help. We feel a responsibility to future generations to leave the place in at least as good condition as we found it, but are concerned that we will not.

It is up to us to create a healthy environment for ourselves and those we love. Perhaps more importantly, it is up to us to pass on a healthy legacy to our future generations.

By living green you can begin to be part of the solution through your practical everyday actions.

I've been given a second chance and want to use it wisely. My family has made the decision to apply simple sustainability to every area of our lives. And although we're by no means perfect, we are on a path that leads us closer to optimal health with every step.

How about you? Are you ready to live greener, healthier and more in harmony with the environment?

If so, congratulations—and welcome to the sustainability revolution.

Jordan Rubin
Founder of Garden of Life
New York Times bestselling author
of *The Maker's Diet*

ACKNOWLEDGEMENTS

THIS BOOK IS THE RESULT of a lifetime of exposure—in person and in print—to great thinkers and inspiring role models for sustainable living.

Leaders of the early environmental movement, whose foresight at a time when natural resources seemed unlimited, left us with a world worth preserving. The current sustainability revolution from organic farming to energy conservation is simply a natural extension of their visionary thinking and decisive actions.

I have learned much from my friends Randy Repass and Mitchell May, both of whom live completely off the grid with their wonderful families and still run great companies, and from Jordan and Nicki Rubin, whose commitment to healthy living is extraordinary.

As an avid health food store shopper, I want to acknowledge the thousands of retailers who make distributing products that can make a difference and sharing their benefits with interested consumers the mission of their working lives.

The scores of companies who are striving to make a difference with the products they sell and by the way they do business continually humble and inspire me as a business person and as an advocate for sustainability. All companies mentioned in this book are there because they are, in my opinion, the best at what they do and for the inspiration they provide. Besides Garden of Life, I have no economic ties to any of them, except paying full retail for their excellent products as an impassioned customer.

Creating this book was a team effort involving research, documentation, writing, editing, design and production. It would not have come together at all without the highly competent assistance of Kathleen Barnes, Tom Foerstel, Roberta Modena, David Steinman, and my various friends and family who provided feedback and much-needed criticism throughout the project.

Finally, ever since we met on her very first day of college, my brilliant and energetic wife Laura's commitment to living a purposeful life has served as a constant source of inspiration.

TABLE OF CONTENTS

INTRODUCTION

GLOBAL WARMING. High gas prices. The organic boom. Climate change. Celebrities driving Priuses. Killer storms. Overflowing landfills. Species extinction.

Skim the headlines of any newspaper or turn on the television for five minutes and it's there. We are using up irreplaceable resources at an alarming rate and poisoning our environment. It just can't go on, and we all know it. That's why green is now a major force in our popular culture and a growing force in our society. Green is even patriotic. Green is the new red, white and blue. It's driving our politics. It's the new big issue—in fact for some it's the ONLY issue.

It is clear to even the casual observer that to make things better requires constructive action. Millions of motivated people want to *do something*. They want to live more sustainable lives. That's what being "green" is all about. They want to leave the planet in livable shape for their kids and grandkids. They want to act on their good intentions.

So, what can you do to make a difference?

That's the question that this book answers. Each chapter addresses a different aspect of sustainability, providing an overview of the issue and practical action steps for making a concrete difference.

Rather than doom, gloom and theory, this is a book that can empower positive personal action. Here at last is a primer on being green that offers practical everyday steps we can take to improve our health and the health of our planet. This easy-to-digest guide is the place to start, with the information structured around the most interesting green topics. A resource guide in the back lets you go deeper and stay informed.

You can pick what interests you the most and get started.

To make that easier, I've divided the book into three parts: Sustainable Health, Sustainable Home, and A Sustainable Future. Here's what you'll learn chapter by chapter and step by step:

Sustainability is keeping a good thing going, whether it's your own health or the planet that we call home. Chapter One introduces the philosophy behind the sustainability movement and inspires participation in this positive and revolutionary new way of life.

SUSTAINABLE HEALTH

For many people, personal health is the first step toward sustainability. Chapter Two makes a compelling case for seven steps to sustain health from the inside, starting with the switch to organic food.

What we put on our bodies can be just as important as what we eat. Chapter Three offers five tips for improving health sustainability by making simple changes to what touches your body. Tips cover organic fiber clothing, safe children's clothing, green dry cleaning, filtering pure water, and the case for natural personal care.

SUSTAINABLE HOME

In the second part, we cover sustainability in the home. Chapter Four covers making your home a healthier, safer and more sustainable place for you and your family, with simple choices that can make a big difference. This chapter provides seven steps to creating a healthier environment for your family at home, including home cleaning products, home energy conservation, waste reduction and recycling, furnishings that help you breathe easier, replacing wasteful disposables, and the benefits of natural lawn care.

Sustainable building and retrofitting are next in Chapter Five. This chapter provides tips and resources for building or remodeling a home to make it as "green" and nontoxic as possible. Topics include design, energy efficiency, sustainable building materials, carpets and flooring, and interior finishes for creating a healthy environment from the ground up.

A SUSTAINABLE FUTURE

Many people identify sustainability with reducing our dependence on fossil fuels. We discuss energy sustainability in Chapter Six, covering practical steps for reducing our impact on our greater environment, as well as reducing our contribution to global warming and climate change. These steps include offsetting your net carbon footprint to zero in about five minutes, renewable power, improving energy efficiency, saving fuel with your existing vehicle and the case for switching to a higher-efficiency car.

Chapter Seven brings it all together, laying out the implications of our consumer participation in the global economy, underscoring how the choices we make impact the sustainability of our planet's health.

Welcome to a new way of life.

Greg Horn
Lighthouse Point, Florida
September 2006

PART I

Sustainable
Health

CHAPTER 1

A New Way of Life

"A journey of one thousand miles starts with a single step."
—Chinese Proverb

AS I EASED MY KAYAK over the glassy ocean swells this morning, I glanced down to see vibrant reefs teeming with fish. Just behind me was the urban center of Fort Lauderdale, Florida, and straight ahead was the deep blue Atlantic. Seeing an urban outline and a vast wilderness in one sweeping view under a brilliant Florida sky turned my thoughts to the relationship between people and our environment. My enjoyment of the natural wonderland I call home was tinged with concern in the knowledge that everything I was experiencing, from the air I was breathing to the level of the sea gliding beneath me, might be radically different in just a few decades.

By now it requires no great scientific insight to understand that resources such as clean air and water, once viewed as unlimited, are in increasingly short supply. We are burning irreplaceable fossil fuels as a basis of our economy, and the carbon released from this burning is now indisputably warming the planet. We are using powerful chemicals to grow and preserve our food, and those chemicals remain in the soil and in our bodies for long periods of time.

But there is reason to be optimistic. People by the millions are searching for ways to live more lightly on the planet, to reduce wastefulness and over-consumption, and to leave the place in good shape for our children, grandchildren and beyond. In small but important ways, they are trying to live their lives differently.

"*What can I do?*"

That's the question I hear most often.

The people I meet in health food stores, at health and nutrition conferences, at gyms or even on airplanes want to live healthier, last longer and make a difference with their lives. They care about the health of their families and their planet and they typically have very good intentions. Most want to live as lightly on the planet as practical.

They just want to know what they can do.

They ask me that question because of my unique background. For two decades, I have combined passion and profession in the healthy living business. As a teen, I discovered the connection between health and nutrition when I dropped most sugar from my diet and felt the difference for myself.

After graduate school, I started as a product manager at General Nutrition Centers. With a combination of new stores, committed franchises, a great team and innovative new supplement products, GNC grew to become the largest specialty retailer of nutrition products in the world. I was promoted from the product development role into sales and marketing, and ultimately became President and CEO of the world's largest specialty nutrition retailer with more than 5,500 stores in 29 countries, in my early thirties.

Following the acquisition of GNC by global nutrition giant Royal Numico, I was heading the parent company's combined $2.5 billion global nutrition business, with operations around the world and nutrition research facilities on three continents.

I was not yet 35 years old and on top of the world.

Then my new corner office in our brand-new downtown headquarters building changed everything.

Soon after moving into our gleaming, 14-story corporate headquarters in downtown Pittsburgh, I developed "sick building syndrome." Initially, my major symptoms were burning eyes and lungs, and headaches. My condition was caused by invisible volatile gases that leach from new synthetic carpets, wall coverings, and most office furniture. Also known as "multiple chemical sensitivity," sick building syndrome is characterized by the loss of the body's ability to handle synthetic chemicals. This loss of tolerance created a wide range of symptoms, including burning eyes, skin rash, loss of concentration, headaches, achy joints and worse, before I was able to start finding solutions.

I discovered my local natural grocery store and started eating organic foods whenever possible. Within weeks, my diet of natural meats, organic fruit and grains, and unprocessed whole foods dramatically improved my energy and digestive health. Not only was this food far healthier, it tasted better too! Eating organic was easy to embrace.

At the office, the first priority was to remove all of the sources of chemicals in my environment. For me, this involved replacing all of the office furniture, changing to a natural carpet and opening the windows in my office. I was fortunate that GNC allowed all of this and my condition improved dramatically once these changes were made.

At home, I gave away any furniture that was made of pressboard or other materials that could release gases into the air. This included my new mattress. I had been sleeping on a brand-new, top-of-the-line mattress and, after a lifetime of being a high-energy early riser, suddenly I could barely function in the morning. I learned the hard way that modern mattresses in the U.S. are made of a substance called formaldehyde-urea foam and sprayed with flame retardants. These flame retardants are banned in many European countries because of the health risks, but flame-retardant treatment is required by law for most mattresses sold in the U.S. I added an organic cotton bed to my "chemical abatement" program and slept on the floor for a month until it came.

I will never forget the morning after my first night sleeping on that organic bed. My breathing was deep, I was totally relaxed and I slept for nine uninterrupted hours for the first time since childhood. I awoke feeling as though I had been on vacation for a week.

My wife, Laura, set out to make our home healthier. Applying her genius to the challenge, she became an expert at practical sustainability in her own right. She embraced our new "greener" lifestyle program with enthusiasm, and changed everything from the products we bought to the way we cleaned our house and cared for our yard. It worked. Now, almost a decade later, I am eating, breathing, and sleeping well. Successfully managing this serious case of multiple chemical sensitivities changed my life for the better, and led me to focus on organic and sustainability issues. I am now fortunate to serve as CEO of Garden of Life, an innovative organic food and nutrition company committed to the path of sustainability in its products and its business practices.

Those were my first steps on a very long road. Like many people who start down this path, my initial interest in sustainability was sparked by a desire to improve my own health. I had literally changed my life. Once I began feeling better, it dawned on me that the ripple effect of a healthy lifestyle is far reaching—onto the fields of organic farms and into the atmosphere we all breathe. I wanted to do more and to think bigger. Like you, I had good intentions.

This book is about acting on those good intentions.

We live at a unique time in human history. Never before have we had so much freedom to make positive choices about our lives. We can choose where we live, what we eat, what we buy and even what we think and believe. More than any time in history, we have the luxury of thinking through the downstream implications of our actions and of changing our behaviors based on our values. This consciousness of cause and effect between our lifestyles—even our diets—and the planet's health is the driving force behind the sustainability movement.

Even if you are just buying organic milk for your kids, your journey has begun.

This new consciousness is also driving our purchasing preferences—making organic food products, fuel-efficient vehicles, and fair-trade products popular beyond the ability of companies to supply all that is demanded. People are demanding a higher standard from their products, their companies, and the quality of their lives.

Sustainability is a value at the core of a new way of life. It is a value that city dwellers and suburbanites alike share with the small organic farmers who grow their food. It is a value that can make life better for all of us and for the island-planet on which we live.

So, what is living green and how can you get started?

In sustainable living, we are looking for a way to live lightly on our planet and pass it on intact—or even better than we found it—to our children and grandchildren and their children and grandchildren.

Why is this important? Because we simply cannot continue doing what we are doing.

Each day we lose 50 to 100 species of animals and plants as they are driven to extinction by human influences.

Each week Americans, representing 5 percent of the world's population, comprise 25 percent of the world's consumption of resources. Much of this consumption ends up discarded as needless waste in our landfills or incinerated into our air, with devastating long-term health and environmental consequences.

In a single year, we send 500 million tons of solid hazardous waste to landfills and pump 3 million tons of toxic chemicals into the air and water.

Each individual person living in our country puts an average of more than 24 tons of carbon, the major greenhouse gas, into the atmosphere each year just from the activities of our modern lifestyle.

The human cost is high even now with diet- and pollution-related ailments on the rise. The long-term stakes are even higher as we use up irreplaceable natural resources while making the planet less hospitable to life. Something has to change.

But change requires courage and action.

No, we don't have to retreat to cabins in the woods and start riding horses to work in order to accomplish this. Instead, we need to find new ways of growth that don't (literally) poison the well.

From the outset, I want to be clear that I am still learning how to make my life more sustainable, while fully participating in the consumer economy. I drive to work every day and we run our air conditioning in the summer. Even with my personal passion for wellness and lingering chemical sensitivities, I travel for business in the middle seat, stay in hotels with cloistered indoor air, and eat at restaurants. It is a top priority for me to make mindful choices about how and when I do those things—but I still have to do them. For me, it's about being practical and thoughtful while living a full life.

A PHILOSOPHY WITH A FUTURE

Sustainable development has been succinctly defined by the World Commission on Environment and Development as, "the ability of humanity to ensure that it meets the needs of the present without compromising the ability of future generations to meet their own needs."

This is not a new idea. Native Americans believed they were stewards of the earth. Ownership of land was a foreign concept to them. The Iroquois Confederacy, a semi-democratic form of government that lasted roughly 700 years, held as one of its guiding principles: "In our every deliberation, we must consider the impact of our decisions on the next seven generations." That was about eight generations ago.

Sustainability as a defining value for a new way of life helps to shape our consciousness of the twenty-first century, but the basic premise has its roots in the mid-nineteenth century transcendentalist movement of Henry David Thoreau and Ralph Waldo Emerson. Thoreau and Emerson's cautions to revere nature, and that to challenge the natural order would eventually order would eventually imperil humankind, were carried forward into the twentieth century by such giants of the environmental movement as John Muir and Aldo Leopold. Yet these founders of modern-day environmentalism took their inspiration, at least in part, from the spiritually based earth consciousness of indigenous people throughout the world, who saw themselves and their natural environment as partners in survival, not as enemies in a war for dominance.

Reaching back seven generations or more into our past, we can easily find the logical next step in our collective consciousness: the knowledge that small individual actions taken now can make a large, long-term difference in our health, the health of our families, our communities and our planet.

YOU'RE NOT ALONE

Most of us think of revolution in violent terms: weapons, bloodshed, overthrow of existing power structures. As I contemplated the concept of a sustainability revolution, I realized the word is appropriate, even if this one is a velvet-glove revolution.

In *The Sustainability Revolution* (New Society Publishers, 2005), Andres Edwards says this is not a revolution of confrontation, but one of consensus "in which the legitimate interests of all parties can be satisfied to a greater or lesser extent, always within the framework of concern for equity."

We're not marching into the streets armed and angry. Instead, we are living our lives differently: quietly taking our trash to recycling centers, buying organic produce, paying a little extra for fair-trade coffee, driving more fuel-efficient cars, such as hybrids, and refusing to buy overpackaged goods.

Even more importantly, we are joining together in coffee shops and in living rooms, in corporate boardrooms and in local public meetings and sharing the message of sustainability with our friends, families, colleagues and neighbors through our actions.

We are already starting to make a difference.

Sustainability is a journey, and as the "eighth generation" we are just taking our first steps. We won't see true sustainability in our lifetimes and our children are unlikely to find full sustainability either.

Yet, for every single plastic bottle of water we refuse to buy, for every chemical we choose not to spray on our lawns or gardens, and for every organic apple or chicken or for every energy-saving appliance we buy, we are creating change.

Buying a hybrid car isn't the perfect choice, but it may be the best choice we have right now. By starting with practical actions we are bringing a new consciousness to our way of living; this revolution is spreading swiftly. The sustainability revolution is an entirely new paradigm, non-hierarchical and unlike any revolution in the history of the world.

Several forces are coming together to make this true. We have better communications systems worldwide, the need for action is more obvious, and we have a much higher level of basic literacy and education worldwide than we have had at any other revolutionary time in history. Good news travels fast nowadays. As we find more sustainable solutions, they can be adopted much more rapidly than was possible even 25 years ago.

Because our lifestyles now have such an impact on the planet, small actions can have large downstream impacts. This guide will give you specific and practical steps you can take in your own life to improve your personal sustainability, as well as that of our society and environment. The goal is to introduce you gently to a whole new way of life, one small step at a time.

A journey of one thousand miles begins with a single step.

I invite you to join the millions who are part of the sustainability revolution and take that first, simple step.

GETTING STARTED: THE TOP TEN

If you want to get started now, pick something worthwhile from the top ten sustainable steps below. Notice the tremendous impact that even small changes in our choices can have.

1. **Eating organic:** For each 1 percent increase in organic food consumption in the U.S. alone, pesticide and herbicide use is reduced by over 10 million pounds per year. Organic food also tastes better and is far healthier than conventional food. And it is probably available at the same store you are shopping in today.

2. **Going carbon zero:** For about $99 per year through nonprofit carbonfund.org, you can offset your entire carbon footprint (the amount of this key greenhouse gas produced through your life activities) with that organization's contributions to renewable power, energy efficiency, and reforestation projects. It won't take you more than about five minutes.

3. **Recycling:** The average person in the U.S. produces 1,609 pounds of waste each year. Recycling can cut that waste stream by up to 75 percent. If each of us recycled just paper, glass and metal, we would save 162 million tons of material from entering American landfills each year. And recycling the enormous amounts of plastics we use each day can save even more.

4. **Denying disposables:** "Disposable" is literally a dirty word. If we all just used a glass instead of a water bottle and a coffee mug instead of a Styrofoam cup, we would save 244 billion bottles and cups made from petrochemical-based plastics from entering the U.S. waste stream each year, and save money at the same time.

5. **Switching to natural personal care:** Using natural personal care has a double benefit—keeping toxic chemicals off your body and then keeping them out of the environment after they wash off your body. Remember, if you wouldn't eat it, don't put it on your body.

6. **Using natural lawn care:** The average suburban lawn uses six times the hazardous chemicals per acre than conventional farming. And your kids and pets play on that lawn. If just 10 percent of us switched to natural lawn care, over half a billion pounds of synthetic fertilizers, pesticides and herbicides would be prevented from entering the environment. And our kids' bodies.

7. **Cleaning green:** Those household chemicals that you have to lock up from children are hazardous to your health. Collectively, we dump 32 million pounds of toxic chemistry down our drains each day, just from household cleaning chemicals. That doesn't count what goes into our indoor air. Switching to green alternatives from your natural supermarket keeps these chemicals out of our bodies and out of our water supply.

8. **Filtering your tap water:** Filtering your tap water to remove chlorine and fluoride provides pure, clean, great-tasting drinking water at a fraction of the cost or environmental impact of expensive and wasteful bottled water that costs more per gallon than gasoline. The payback on a $60 water filter takes only a few weeks for most households. As an added benefit, there is no plastic bottle to leach harmful phthalates (which act like estrogens in the body) into your water.

   Making small, individual changes can lead to broad, sweeping changes that will allow us to sustain ourselves for generations to come.

9. **Increasing energy efficiency:** Energy and fuel efficiency can dramatically reduce use of fossil fuels. Insulate your home and consider a hybrid next time you buy a car. The investment in efficiency pays off rapidly in lower fuel and energy costs.

10. **Staying informed:** Knowledge empowers informed action. Subscribe to one of the many green magazines or visit www.wellbuilding.com regularly to stay informed on sustainability developments, resources, tips and tools.

This book is designed to give you simple and practical tools to help yourself and to help heal our planet. Each chapter addresses a different aspect of sustainability, providing an overview of the issue and practical action steps for making a meaningful difference. In the first few chapters, you will learn how personal health choices are linked to the health of our environment and to sustain greater personal health by incorporating sustainability into what goes into and onto your body. Later chapters expand the discussion beyond personal health to the environments in which we live—first our buildings, then our planet. Finally, we will examine the broader implications of the sustainability revolution for the world around us.

What You Need To Know

- Our diet and lifestyle choices have a direct cause-and-effect relationship with the health of the planet. Buying an organic apple has a ripple effect all the way back to the worms in the soil that nourished that apple tree.
- You can be a catalyst of change as one person. Together we can make huge strides to make the world greener.
- Making small, individual changes can lead to broad, sweeping changes that will allow us to sustain ourselves for generations to come.
- We are already making progress. Thanks to consumer pressure, there are generations that don't remember that McDonald's hamburgers ever came in Styrofoam containers. Countless birth defects and deaths from cancer have undoubtedly been prevented by the banning of DDT and PCBs, and municipal recycling programs have kept uncountable tons of slow-to-biodegrade plastic, Styrofoam and toxic chemicals out of our landfills.

CHAPTER 2

Sustaining Health from the Inside

"Let food be your medicine."
– Hippocrates

I WILL NEVER FORGET my first visit to a really large-scale farm—it was on a warm September day in Watsonville, California. I was born in Iowa and my grandparents always had a farm that we visited as children, but this was different. First, this farm was enormous, totaling several hundred acres. Instead of the well-tended (and hand-weeded) rows of corn and beans I had seen as a child, this farm had just one crop: lettuce almost as far as the eye could see.

Standing in that huge field of lettuce, I thought of all the salads and sandwiches those bright green leaves would adorn. As I was marveling at this vast field of green, I noticed that the field workers wore thick gloves, long sleeves and rubber boots. Some wore masks over their faces. I asked the owner of the farm why the protective clothing was needed, and forgot all about my next salad. He told me that lettuce was sprayed an average of 12 times with up to 50 different pesticides, fungicides and herbicides before it reached your local salad bar. Rubber boots and gloves were protecting the workers from the chemicals that you and I eat every day!

For me, visiting this farm made the connection between my own diet and the health of the planet. Cause and effect was clear: I was creating demand for pesticides and poisoned soil every time I bought lettuce that used these chemicals. Worse yet, I had been feeding them to my family!

This was also right about the time when I began incorporating organic food into my diet to regain my health. I was worried about my own personal health sustainability and had to take care of myself out of necessity. Because this was my big, first step into the "green movement" more than 10 years ago, here is where our journey begins.

Think about the synergy that can exist between what is good for each of us as individuals and what is good for our planet.

This can be a very positive connection. In case after case, what is good for you is ultimately good for society and good for our world. For example, eating organic foods reduces your personal exposure to harmful chemical pesticides. Eating sustainably caught wild salmon gives you a great source of good fats essential to overall health while reducing the demand for farmed salmon, which have been shown to be contaminated with a variety of industrial pollutants.

Drinking pure water from your home or office filtration system keeps toxins, especially heavy metals, out of your system and keeps billions of plastic bottles out of our landfills.

And creating consumer demand for organically grown fruits and vegetables is a commitment to the healthiest food possible while sustaining farmers who are committed to building healthy soil, conserving water and reducing the use of pesticides and synthetic fertilizers that are contaminating food and water supplies.

Committing yourself to your own health is your first step toward a more sustainable life.

A SUSTAINABLE DIET

It may sound ironic, but most of us take the first step toward personal sustainability with our mouths.

WHAT YOU CAN DO—
7 Steps to Sustainable Eating

1. Buy organic whenever possible
2. Be careful of fish
3. Eat low on the food chain
4. Filter your water
5. Reduce sugar and sodas
6. Cut fried and processed foods
7. Change your cup

Sustainable Step #1:
Buy organic whenever possible

Going organic is perhaps the simplest and most important first step you take toward sustaining your health and improving the environment at the same time.

You can start tomorrow with a trip to your local natural supermarket. What could be easier than that?

Typical foods are grown in soils that have been chemically fertilized and sprayed with multiple herbicides (chemicals that kill unwanted plants) and pesticides (chemicals that kill insects), then processed with high heat and preservative chemicals to extend shelf life and added sugars to improve taste, and packaged in disposable plastic containers for your convenience. For example, the typical bag of potato chips you buy at the supermarket has been subjected to over 50 chemicals from seed to shelf and can contain up to 75 times the "safe" levels of cancer-causing acrylamide established by the state of California.

The current organic boom is a consumer reaction to the potentially toxic stuff used in making our food. Both common sense and research confirm that eating organic is healthier, and that kids who eat primarily organic diets have far lower levels of pesticides in their bodies than those who eat a standard American diet.

How can you explain the fact that the dramatic rise of modern illnesses, such as digestive health problems, heart disease and all types of cancers, coincides precisely with the widespread introduction of the modern diet? There are two possible explanations: 1) changes in our biological machinery or 2) changes in the inputs. Our bodies are incredible machines that can turn food into fuel to sustain us. Since the machinery has not changed in the last 100 years, that leaves the input as the culprit. And our food inputs have changed dramatically in the last century.

At the close of World War II, chemical companies had learned plenty about how to kill living things with chemicals. With surpluses of these chemicals left over from the war and chemical plants running at full speed, they literally applied that knowledge to our food—adapting chemical toxins to poison insects that ate some of the farmers' crops. Farmers were lured by the promises of greater yields. (These were empty promises, as it turns out. In 1989, crop loss to insects was about one-third, the same as in 1915.) The surplus toxins were sprayed on our food. They kept on spraying to the present day, when 15 or more chemicals can be applied to a single crop during its growing season. These chemical residues remain on your food, and in your body, with unknown—but probably not good—results.

It's a sad truth: We are living in world where 70,000 new chemicals have been introduced in just the last 100 years. Many of these end up in our food. In fact, the average American consumes about 14 pounds of chemicals a year just from additives like artificial food colorings, flavorings, emulsifiers and preservatives; 2 pounds of the 14 are synthetic chemicals from residues on conventional food, such as pesticides, herbicides, antibiotics, hormones and heavy metals. As a result of our conventional diets, each of us has an average of 500 manmade chemicals circulating in our blood. Children are especially at risk because they are smaller and have developing metabolic systems.

Disgusting!

The Environmental Protection Agency (EPA) now considers 60 percent of all herbicides (weed killers), 90 percent of all fungicides (mold killers) and 30 percent of all insecticides (insect killers) as potentially cancer-causing.

Is this unprecedented toxic load a reason that cancers, liver and kidney diseases, birth defects, brain diseases and other once-rare malfunctions are rising at such an alarming rate? No one knows for sure, but chemical exposures are a known risk factor for all of these diseases. Even the EPA ranks pesticide residue exposure as the third-highest risk factor for cancer out of the 29 environmental problems that it regulates. Only industrial chemical exposure for workers and indoor radon exposure rank higher.

Dr. Walter Crinnion, N.D., of Seattle's Bastyr University, the premier naturopathic institution in the nation, wrote in the 1995 *Organic Gardening Almanac* that he tested a patient for 18 of the more common pesticide residues and found the patient had 9 of them in his blood, including active DDT. Although DDT was a banned in 1972, it is amazingly persistent in the soil. Residues of this pesticide, believed to cause cancer, liver toxicity and fertility problems, are still quite common.

"If he had 50 percent of the chemicals we tested for, how many did he have that we didn't test for? Unfortunately, out of 70,000 chemicals in current daily use in this country, only about 250 can be tested for in humans," Dr. Crinnion wrote.

Organic foods are grown without the use of synthetic pesticides, synthetic fertilizers, antibiotics or added hormones. That means safer food without the chemical load of conventionally grown food. Organic farmers work to improve the ecology of their soils, resulting in healthier plants and more nutritious fruits and vegetables. Look for the USDA certification seal on the package to be sure the food you are buying is organic.

Following is a list of the conventional foods that have the highest levels of contamination from pesticides, herbicides, hormones, antibiotics or heavy metals. If you can simply shift to buying organic versions of these common foods as a start, you will have made big strides toward cleaning up your diet and your health.

Getting Started:
The Top 10 Foods to Buy Organic

1. **Meats:** These are high on the food chain, and thus can concentrate chemicals from the animals' diets in their fatty tissues.
2. **Dairy products:** Also high on the food chain and rich in fats, which is where harmful chemicals become stored.
3. **Fish:** While not strictly organic, it is critical to buy wild fish and avoid all farmed fish, which can contain high levels of contaminants. Hint: All "Atlantic salmon" is farmed, as this fish is virtually extinct in the wild.
4. **Berries:** Strawberries, raspberries and other berries including grapes have a thin, absorbent skin that you eat. These fruits are heavily sprayed and tend to absorb more of the chemicals that they come in contact with during production.
5. **Salad crops:** Lettuce, spinach and celery are highly sprayed, and have no outer shell to protect the part you eat—the leaf.

If you can't go organic all at once, begin buying high-priority organic foods when you can. Organic food also contains higher levels of key nutrients, so you will be improving your nutrition while reducing your intake of pesticides and herbicides.

You can also find good, healthy food for much lower prices at your local farmer's market. It may not be officially labeled "organic," but if you talk to the sellers, you'll find much local produce is grown without pesticides, herbicides and artificial fertilizers.

Look for foods that are minimally packaged, since packaging of food accounts for about 7 percent of its total energy consumption.

You'll want to avoid those Styrofoam trays and plastic wrappings that might outgas into the food. Meats wrapped in paper, veggies carried

6. **Mushrooms:** Mushrooms are highly absorbent, and conventional growing uses powerful fungicides between crops to keep stray species from invading the intended crop.

7. **Root crops:** Conventional potatoes, yams, carrots, onions and other root crops can be sprayed with fungicides as well as pesticides, and the parts you eat grow in direct contact with the chemicals.

8. **Bananas:** Banana plantations use up to 20 times more pesticides per acre than crops grown in industrialized countries. Conventional bananas are often grown with a blue plastic bag of pesticides placed over the soft, absorbent skin of the fruit. Enough said?

9. **Waxed fruit:** That shiny apple has a wax coating that locks in the pesticides and makes them very difficult to wash off.

10. **Coffee and Tea:** Technically not "foods," but hot-water brewing can concentrate the residual pesticides used in the growing process while it is extracting the "good stuff." Remember to use an unbleached filter and to avoid the Styrofoam cup like a plague!

home in your own cloth bag, and dairy products in glass or paper containers are your best choices.

Sustainable Step #2:
Be careful of fish

I think fish is worth consuming in moderation—but only certain less polluted species and, even then, not more than two servings a week.

Cold water fatty fish is an excellent source of omega-3 fatty acids, but it can also be a source of environmental toxins, including mercury. The government has recently issued warnings against consuming too much fish, especially for pregnant women.

Sadly, most of the fish available on North American markets comes from industrial fish farms that can not only pollute our waterways, but can also pollute our bodies.

In a landmark 2002 study, Canadian researchers found that a single serving of farmed salmon contains three to six times the World Health Organization's daily intake limit for dioxin and polychlorinated biphenyls. Dioxin is produced as a result of manufacturing with chlorine processes, such as bleached paper products. PCBs (polychlorinated biphenyls), chemicals once used in the manufacture of electrical and heating equipment, paints, plastics, rubbers, dyes and many other substances, were banned in 1977 after the U.S. EPA called them "probable human carcinogens."

A single serving of farmed salmon contains three to six times the World Health Organization's daily intake limit for dioxin and PCBs.

In its December 26, 2005, issue, *U.S. News and World Report* reported that farmed salmon are raised on fish pellets that are often contaminated with PCBs.

Because farmed fish live in unnaturally close quarters, antibiotics are fed to the fish to prevent disease. The use of antibiotics is particularly hazardous to the health of human beings (and even fish, long term) since it promotes the spread of antibiotic resistance.

Farmers dose their captive fish with a potent anti-parasitic drug called ivermectin to rid them of sea lice. This pharmaceutical makes it into the waterways, where it is known to kill some species of shrimp.

The FDA (Food and Drug Administration) says that all women who are pregnant or may become pregnant, nursing mothers, and young children should abstain completely from shark, swordfish, king mackerel and tilefish because of the high levels of mercury contamination that may be particularly harmful to unborn babies and the developing nervous systems of young children.

A continuously updated list of fish that is naturally low in toxins is available at The Monterey Bay Aquarium's Seafood Watch service: www.mbayaq.org/cr/seafoodwatch.asp. This excellent service is updated regularly as fish species safety changes, and provides a simple "green, yellow, red" rating system and a guide to local safe seafood sources.

Sustainable Step #3:
Eat low on the food chain

Big fish eat little fish, and little fish eat tiny fish, and tiny fish eat plankton. In general, the larger and longer-lived the animal, the greater the toxic load of that animal. A 20-year-old swordfish has many times the level of environmental pollutants as a four-month-old sardine. So, to minimize the negatives, eating low on the food chain only makes sense.

Unless you are a vegetarian, I recommend making animal protein—whether it's fish, meat, poultry or dairy products—an occasional part of your diet rather than the "main event" of the meal in order to help reduce your overall chemical load and to reduce the load on the planet.

The average American eats 209 pounds of meat a year. That's a lot of beef, and it takes a lot of water to produce. Consider how much it costs to produce just one pound of meat:

- For grain-fed beef: 10 pounds of grain and 2,700 gallons of water
- For ranch-raised beef: as much as 5,000 gallons of water per pound
- For pork: four pounds of grain
- For chicken: two pounds of grain

By contrast, it takes about 21 gallons of water to produce one pound of tomatoes and roughly the same amount to produce a pound of potatoes or wheat. Even rice, the most water-consuming grain, requires only one-tenth of the amount of water per pound compared to the water requirements of beef.

Meat production is also land-hungry. An equivalent amount of land can feed six times the number of people on a plant-based diet than people eating a meat-based diet.

Reducing your consumption of meat and other animal products is a positive step for your health and the health of the planet.

Sustainable Step #4:
Filter your water

Food is important, but you can only survive three days without water. Water is essential to all plant and animal life and it's no accident that water is the most plentiful substance on the planet and in our bodies.

In recent years, we've become more conscious of our need for water—to the point where we Americans consumed nearly 7 billion gallons of bottled water in 2004. That's eight ounces of bottled water per day for every man, woman and child!

How do we get quality water when the tap water in most cities contains chlorine (a broad-spectrum antimicrobial), traces of metals like arsenic, lead and aluminum, and added fluoride that may contribute to hypothyroidism, weakened bones and nerve damage?

The answer for many of us has been bottled water. But that's the wrong answer!

First, in terms of personal health, those flexible plastic water bottles are a source of phthalates, an impossible-to-pronounce group of petrochemicals that has been shown in animal studies to emasculate male offspring and to cause early puberty and reproductive malfunctions in females. Chemicals that disrupt hormonal systems are called "endocrine disrupters," and phthalates are estrogenic endocrine disrupters, meaning that they mimic the powerful female hormone estrogen in the body. This is not good. In men, this can mean lower sperm counts, decreased sex drive, lower energy and feminizing effects. In women, phthalates and other estrogenic endocrine disrupters are linked to early puberty and increased rates of breast and ovarian cancers.

In fact, human sperm counts in the U.S. have dropped by 50 percent over the past century. No one knows why for sure, but estrogenic phthalates from plastics and synthetic growth hormones in conventional milk are the most likely culprits. The average American girl is now reaching puberty a full 18 months earlier than girls of just 50 years ago. Breast development has been seen in girls as young as 24 months. Again, estrogen-mimicking phthalates are strongly suspected.

University of North Carolina researchers offered this explanation for early puberty after their study showed more than 48 percent of African-American girls and 14.7 percent of Caucasian girls had entered puberty by the age of eight—much earlier than the previous generation: "The possibility that the increasing use of certain plastics and insecticides that degrade into substances that have estrogen-related physiological effects on living things should be investigated in relation to the earlier onset of puberty."

The longer the water is in contact with the plastic, or if the water is heated in the bottle, as when you leave it in your car, the higher the level of phthalates that have leached into the water. The older the bottle, the more phthalates are released, so if you're thinking you're being environmentally conscious by re-using your plastic bottles, think again about your health. Don't use those plastic water bottles more than twice. Better yet, don't use them at all.

Studies have shown that most bottled water in this $22 billion industry in the U.S. is no better than tap water, and some is even worse. There are far fewer regulations on bottled water both in the U.S. and in Europe than on tap water, so there have been cases where bottled water has actually been shown to be more contaminated than tap water.

It's an expensive habit we've created—hard on our pocketbooks and hard on our planet.

The economic cost is enormous: Bottled water costs up to 1,000 times as much as tap water. What's more, bottled water costs more to transport than tap water—1.5 billion gallons of fuel oil annually, enough to fuel 10,000 cars for an entire year—while tap water is delivered through an energy-efficient infrastructure. That oil use does not include the petro-chemicals required to manufacture all of those plastic bottles. We com-plain about spending $3 for a gallon of gasoline, but walk from the pump to the counter to pay three times as much per gallon for a bottle of water!

Worse yet, billions upon billions of plastic water bottles are clogging our landfills—1.5 billion tons of plastic a year worldwide—and these plastic bottles will take more than 1,000 years to completely biodegrade.

So, how do we get the clean, pure water we need without damaging the environment or our own health?

The answer is simple and fairly inexpensive: in-house (or in-office) water filtration.

There are several excellent products on the market that can filter all of the water that comes in contact with your body. Some are simple and inexpensive, like a sink-top filter that attaches to your kitchen faucet or a carbon filter for your shower water.

Make sure you pour that clean, filtered water into a glass container, not a plastic cup or bottle. For travel purposes (and for baby bottles and food storage), you have a couple of options. For trips around town, reuse a glass iced tea bottle. You can wash them and use them over and over. When it's not feasible to carry glass bottles, look for hard plastic con-tainers made from:

• Polypropylene, designated "#5 PP"
• High-density polyethylene, designated "#2HDPE"
• Low-density polyethylene, designated "#4 LDPE"

These are not known to leach harmful substances the way that soft plastics do. Just be mindful that even these containers have to be thrown out someday—and they'll live in our landfills forever. Better yet, invest in a stainless steel water bottle from Kleen Kanteen, which you can find at www.greenfeet.com, and avoid plastics altogether.

Note that those colorful Nalgene bottles made from Lexan are not on this list. I used them for years, and thought they were safer because the Lexan polycarbonate did not impart taste to the water. But I was wrong. A 1998 study at Case Western Reserve University by Dr. Patricia Hunt found that Lexan bottles can leach BPA into water at rates high enough to cause genetic defects in the reproductive systems of mice. That was enough for me. The Nalgene company has recently launched HDPE versions of their most popular Lexan products, but since they may look identical, double-check to make sure you are buying the HDPE versions. The material used is imprinted on the bottom of most plastic bottles.

Sustainable Step #5:
Reduce sugars and sodas

I was a typical teenager, eating burgers for lunch and drinking sodas to stay awake on my late-shift summer job. Then I read the book *Sugar Blues* and completely changed my diet. William Dufty's message was clear: Sugar is poison and it is responsible for a large number of our health woes. It was a pretty heavy topic for a 15-year-old, but I was sold. I gave up my junk food diet overnight. I was shocked at how much better I felt after a few more days and began my lifelong fascination with the connection between what we choose to eat and how we feel and live.

Simply giving up sugar will offer you substantial protection against serious health challenges, especially those related to being overweight, including diabetes, heart disease and cancer.

Sugar is one of the most insidious substances in our diets. Refined sugar does not occur in nature, and it tricks your body into overeating and storing fat. Eventually, this long-term trickery burns out the organs responsible for regulating your metabolism and sets the stage for obesity, diabetes, and other life-impairing conditions. As a direct result of sugar in our diets, diabetes and obesity are on the rise in all age groups, including children.

Food researcher Nancy Appleton, Ph.D., author of *Lick the Sugar Habit* (Avery, 1996), lists 146 reasons why sugar is ruining your health. You can read them all on her website: www.nancyappleton.com. But let me just recap a few of the conditions sugar has been scientifically proven to cause or make worse:

- Diabetes
- Obesity
- Immune system suppression
- Mineral imbalances
- Increase in triglycerides (blood fats)
- Hyperactivity in children
- Digestive dysfunction
- Alcoholism

- Arthritis
- Asthma
- Heart disease
- Gallstones
- Osteoporosis
- Some types of cancer
- Cataracts

This is a scary list, considering the average American eats nearly 160 pounds of sugars a year. It certainly scared the wits out of me more than 25 years ago when I was 15. Now I don't touch table sugar and rarely eat anything that has any type of refined sugar in it. I highly recommend reducing sugar to sustain long-term health.

How to spot sugar on a label? Sugar is sugar, whether the product label says it comes from cane sugar, sugar beets, or the much cheaper high fructose corn syrup (HFCS). If you're an avid label reader, you'll find high fructose corn syrup is added to hundreds of foods to enhance flavor.

The average American eats nearly 160 pounds of sugars a year, 40 times more than Americans ate a century ago.

HFCS is a sweetener that is even worse than table sugar. It is a highly processed sweetener from corn syrup that is metabolized in a way that basically deposits its energy directly as body fat. And it is in almost everything. Take a look at this chart, showing the relationship between HFCS consumption and obesity. A picture is worth a thousand words!

If you can do just one thing to improve your personal sustainability, drop all obvious sources of sugar from your diet today.

Obesity and High Fructose Corn Syrup

The number of Americans who are obese has quadrupled in recent years, a study shows. At the same time, high fructose corn syrup consumption has risen at parallel rates.

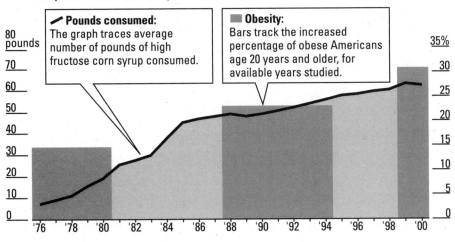

Source: Centers for Disease Control, American Obesity Association, Chronicle research

Sustainable Step #6:
Cut fried and processed foods

Fried food is a major source of excess calories, representing a large portion of the 40 percent of calories from fat in the average American's diet. The next step toward personal sustainability through a better diet is to cut fried foods entirely, and cut back on processed foods.

When a food is fried, it soaks up fat. And, the unnaturally high heat of frying changes the fat molecules into a form that your body has a harder time digesting. This fat ends up in your arteries and around your waist. Fried food is popular because it tastes good and is inexpensive. But simply cutting fried food from your diet and replacing it with baked or grilled foods can cut fat in those foods by up to 75 percent, enough to have a significant impact on your health and weight.

Processed foods almost always use chemical preservatives, additives and flavorings as part of the processing for taste and shelf stability. These foods have a long shelf life and they're convenient, but they give you less for your body to use.

To reduce processed foods, clean out your pantry. Start by getting rid of the white stuff. That pure white color is a sure sign of a food that has been highly refined, often with the use of chemicals and bleaches. Think about it. How many foods in nature are naturally white? Throw out the refined sugar and white flour that is, at best, devoid of nutrition and, at worst, a serious threat to your health.

If you are serious about changing your diet quickly, throw out all boxed foods, mixes, hydrogenated oils, canned soups, crackers, white rice and canned vegetables (except tomatoes and beans—more about them later).

Why? Isn't that a waste of good food? First of all, it's not good food. Give it to the local food bank if it will make you feel better, but consider this:

White flour, white rice, pasta and baked goods made from white flour have had virtually all the nutrients taken out of them in the milling process. True, some nutrients, including folic acid, are added back into them after the nutrient-rich grain polishings are thrown away, but not enough to make them worth eating. In some countries, the grain polishings are fed to pigs, putting the pigs on a better diet than the people who insist on pristine white breads, cakes and rice.

What's more, these foods are made from crops that are heavily sprayed with pesticides and herbicides. Residual amounts inevitably remain in the finished product. If that's not enough to convince you, most baked goods contain hydrogenated fats—the kind that are guaranteed to clog your arteries. Also called trans fatty acids, nutritionists say you should completely eliminate them from your diet.

Conventional processed foods are designed and manufactured for a long shelf life. That means treating the foods with heat and chemicals to remove all bacteria that can cause spoilage. Killing bad bacteria in food is a good thing, but the heat used in processing these foods also kills the beneficial enzymes that help digestion and destroys the natural vitamin content of the foods, making them less nutritious. Chemical preservatives used to extend shelf life remain in the food and can kill beneficial bacteria in your body and can also interact with each other with unintended consequences.

Cereals, cake mixes, and prepared batters are made up of white flour and white sugar as main ingredients. Many prepared mixes have white pasta, dehydrated potatoes or white rice as a base, with high-sodium bouillon, corn starch, artificial flavorings and preservatives, and perhaps a few dried spices for flavor. Ounce for ounce, these mixes are far more expensive than the individual ingredients that take just a few minutes to throw together for a vastly more healthy meal. Boxed foods are near the top of the list of the most highly processed and the least nutritious foods you can find.

Hydrogenated cooking oils, such as Crisco, contain trans fatty acids, which are proven to increase the risk of heart disease. Get rid of any hydrogenated oil that is solid at room temperature. Replace them with olive oil or with coconut oil, which is naturally solid below 75 degrees and very healthy.

Canned vegetables and fruits have had virtually all the nutrients cooked out of them during the canning process, since heat destroys most vitamins. Canned fruits are depleted of nutrients, plus they have added sugar. The exceptions to this rule are canned tomatoes and beans. Cooked tomatoes are an excellent source of lycopene, a carotenoid that has been shown to protect against heart disease and certain types of cancer. Cooking actually breaks down the cell walls, releasing more lycopene into any tomato product and making it healthier than even raw tomatoes. Canned pinto, kidney, black or any other type of beans are huge timesavers and the cooking process does not rob them of important nutrients and fiber.

Sustainable Step #7:

Change your cup

This is my way of saying banish plastics from your home as much as possible.

Plastics are found in almost everything we use in our daily lives. There are plastic vapors in the air we breathe, and the plastic in food packaging can be absorbed into our food. Plastics outgas for the life of these products, but the rate of outgassing diminishes over time.

The most dangerous plastics are phthalate-rich vinyl (vinyl chloride and polyvinyl chloride), the type used in food packaging as well as toys, baby pacifiers and teethers, floor tiles and a wide variety of household products.

Those Styrofoam cups you get with most carry-out coffee not only clog landfills in almost as high numbers as plastic water bottles, the styrene from which the cups are made can cause respiratory problems and even, in extreme cases, respiratory paralysis and death. The EPA classifies styrene as a Class 3 carcinogen, meaning there is limited scientific evidence of its toxicity to both animals and humans. When styrene was inhaled daily by lab animals, there was an increase in breast cancer, lung tumors and leukemia.

Drinking a hot beverage from a styrene-based Styrofoam cup vaporizes the toxic chemical and increases the potential for damage to your health as you breathe in the fumes.

Take a good old china mug to work. If you must stop by the local java shop, ask them to switch to paper-based cups that are biodegradable and emit no styrene fumes, or get them to let you use your own cup.

Finally, never use a microwave oven to heat or reheat any food or beverage in a plastic cup or container. This includes plastic cling wraps often used to cover food in the microwave. The rapid heating in a microwave oven makes the chemicals in plastic many times more volatile and more likely to get into your food or beverage. If you store or transport food in plastic containers, make sure you transfer them to glass or ceramic before heating.

What You Need To Know

- There is a strong connection between the diet you choose to consume and the health of the planet.
- A healthy diet is not only an insurance policy for your personal well-being, it contributes to the well-being of the planet.
- You can reduce your exposure to chemicals in food by eating as low as possible on the food chain.
- Much of our conventional food has been grown or processed with unhealthy additives.
- White is an unhealthy color when it comes to many common foods. Cut as many white foods, such as sugar and white flour, as you can.
- You'll avoid lots of chemicals by buying food in season as close to home as possible.
- Avoid fried, sugared and processed food.
- Eat as much organic food as possible to avoid chemical pesticide residues, hormones and antibiotics on conventional food.
- Minimize plastic touching your food, and never use a microwave oven to heat food in plastic containers.
- Drink clean, filtered water out of glass containers whenever possible.

CHAPTER 3

Sustaining Health from the Outside

"The perception of beauty is a moral test."
—Henry David Thoreau

MY MOTHER NEVER USES SUNSCREEN. Going against the grain throughout my childhood, she has always thought that the sunshine (in moderation) was good for our skin and still does not trust chemicals. I thought she was crazy, and slathered sunscreen on my young daughters to protect their delicate skin from the powerful rays of the Florida sun. Then, in the process of researching potential aggravators of my own conditions, I found out that conventional sunscreens contained potentially harmful chemicals like phthalates and estrogen mimickers that I did not want my daughters to absorb through their skin. Imagine my sense of betrayal, and my surprise that my mother may have been at least partially right. By the way, she is almost 70 and gets regular comments on her great skin. I have found safer sunscreens for my family.

It's not just what you put *in* your body, but what you put *on* it that can have a profound effect on your health and the health of our planet.

It sometimes shocks me to see people who wouldn't dream of eating processed foods slathering on chemically laden moisturizers or sunscreens before taking a hike or a run. What you put on your body is just as important as what you put in it. It's just that many of us don't realize how permeable our skin really is.

Your skin is the largest organ of your body. It is porous, so what you apply to your skin is quickly absorbed into your entire system. Think of your skin more as a sponge than as a barrier.

If you're not sure this is true, try a little experiment.

Take a cut clove of garlic and rub it on the sole of your foot. You will taste garlic in your mouth within 15 minutes. That's how quickly it is absorbed by your skin and travels through your body.

Products that you have used for years and thought were fine might turn out not to be fine at all. Take sunscreen as an example. Thanks to the information in this chapter, you won't need to make the same mistakes I have made. I'll show you how to find personal care and cosmetic products manufactured by companies with sustainability, efficacy and safety as core company values. Once you have this information, it will be easy to switch to more sustainable and equally effective products.

The information here is meant to help you make an informed decision, not to contribute to any sense of being overwhelmed. Only when you are armed with the facts can you protect yourself, your family and your planet.

And you do need to be aware. Leading scientific researchers link the chemical phthalate family, for example, with profound reproductive effects at doses that approximate those typically taken into the body from cosmetic products. Another family of chemicals called parabens is linked with estrogenic effects in cell cultures and traces have been found in breast tumors, but not in healthy tissue.

The good news is that consumers are becoming increasingly aware of the health dangers from these chemicals in certain types of clothing, personal care products and cosmetics. It is important to recognize that some of the most popular cosmetic products are derived largely from petroleum-based ingredients that find their way into rivers, lakes, and the air we breathe. These degrade the environment and cause a decline in sustainability. So, using natural personal care and cosmetic products has the double benefit of being healthier for you and better for the environment we all share.

Mollie's Story

This story from the November 19, 2005, *Daily Mail* tells of a British child whose growing pollution levels in her own tissues are typical of the chemical exposure of children in industrialized nations, including the United States.

At 11, Mollie Clements looks a picture of health.

Yet, tests have found a cocktail of 35 toxic chemicals in Mollie's blood. The dangerous compounds are found in everything from everyday household cleaners and perfumes to saucepans and toys. Many have been linked to cancers, genital abnormalities and birth defects.

Mollie, however, is not alone in having them in her system. She and her parents, from Seaton, Devon (in the United Kingdom), were among seven families who agreed to be tested for 104 manmade chemicals by the World Wildlife Fund. A total of 75 of them were present in children.

Mollie's mother, Sara, 43, had 33 chemicals in her blood while Mollie had 36 from five different groups. Among the chemicals in Mollie's blood were phthalates, which are used in soap, makeup and plastics. These chemicals have been shown to disrupt the development of baby boys' reproductive organs. Perfluorinated compounds, used in nonstick pans and water-resistant clothing, have been linked to cancer. There are also fears that many fire retardants, used in furniture and electrical products, could affect brain development in early life, leading to learning difficulties.

Mollie's blood also contained PCBs, the industrial chemicals linked to liver cancer and male fertility problems, which were banned at least a decade before she was born. She also tested positive for the chemical DDE, formed when the pesticide DDT breaks down in the body.

WHAT YOU CAN DO–
6 Steps for Sustainable Personal Care

1. Choose natural, organic-fiber clothing
2. Don't compromise with your children's clothing
3. Find a greener dry cleaner
4. Buy safe personal care products
5. Filter your shower and bath water
6. Choose natural feminine hygiene

Sustainable Step #1:
Choose natural, organic-fiber clothing

Do something revolutionary: Buy an organic cotton shirt. Cotton is the most intensive pesticide-use crop in the world, accounting for approximately 25 percent of all insecticides used worldwide, although cotton is grown on only 3 percent of the world's farmland. Worse yet, all nine of the top pesticides used on cotton crops in the U.S. are classified by the EPA as Category 1—the most dangerous category of chemicals. Cotton clothing places some of these pesticides right on your skin.

Other common types of clothing aren't much better. Clothing made from synthetic fibers like acrylic, nylon and polyester is coated with formaldehyde finishes that continuously give off minute plastic vapors as the fabric is warmed against your skin, causing unknown effects as well as known problems: allergies and breathing troubles.

It is becoming increasingly easy to find great-looking clothing that is made from 100 percent organic cotton, silk, linen, hemp, or tencel (made from natural cellulose found in wood pulp). Marci Zaroff, an undisputed pioneer and maven of the ECOfashion® world, has worked for 18 years to bust the myth that organic clothing is devoid of style, colorless, scratchy and overpriced.

"People are buying organic clothing because it's beautiful, luxurious and fits well," Zaroff explains. "Who would want to buy a conventional cotton t-shirt when you realize it takes one-third of a pound of pesticides to make one shirt?"

Under the Canopy clothing has been featured on countless television shows and publications ranging from *Newsweek* to *Health Magazine*. With "stars like Cameron Diaz, Daryl Hannah, Sting and Bruce Springsteen sporting Zaroff's clothes, the company is finding its niche among the environmentally conscious of the fashion world," reports a Florida newspaper that featured her work.

"People are so disconnected from leaving the world a better place for the next generation and it's just so unfair and so irresponsible," she told the paper. "But we're giving people products where they don't have to compromise their lifestyle. They don't have to sacrifice style and quality to wear organic clothing."

Zaroff's passion is contagious. "We should all be looking for things that promote health and don't deplete the earth, but instead build it," she says.

Other leaders in organic fiber are Prana and Patagonia. Patagonia (www.patagonia.com) is an outdoor gear company, selling everything from technical climbing gear to high-tech jackets that look great on the mountain or walking your dog to the coffee shop. Patagonia buys ONLY organic cotton for its clothing, and has great-looking organic clothing for men. The company's founder, Yvonne Chouinard, is a pioneer of sustainability and an environmental advocate from way back. Prana (www.prana.com) is a leading brand of yoga and climbing clothing, which grew from the personal interests of its founder, Beaver Theodosakis. This company lives and breathes sustainability—and its line is progressing towards more certified organic and natural fabrics.

Sustainable Step #2:
Don't compromise with your children's clothing

Most of us look at a newborn baby and think how pure their little bodies are, uncorrupted by the pollutants that we adults accumulate. It's a nice thought, but sadly, it's not true. New research shows our kids are now being exposed to pollutants in the womb and many start life with a significant chemical load.

Scientists have long believed that the placenta shields a fetus from pollutants, but a 2005 study conducted by the Environmental Working Group busted that myth by showing traces of 287 chemicals in the umbilical cord blood of 10 infants they studied. Among the toxins were mercury, pesticides and the chemicals used in fire retardants and stain-resistant fabric coatings.

The study's findings generated a great deal of concern since children's smaller brains, developing organs and more permeable tissues put them at greater risk from chemical exposure than adults. In addition, their undeveloped immune systems are themselves vulnerable to permanent damage from some of these pollutants.

"A child's brain is very vulnerable and developing very rapidly *in utero* and during the first two years of life," Jane Houlihan, co-author of the study, told *Newsweek* in July 2005.

Fire-resistant clothing commonly used for children's nightclothes may be a major contributor to the toxic load now being placed on our children. The chemicals used to make the clothing fire retardant are polybrominated diphenyl ether (PBDE), which has been linked to brain and thyroid development problems, and newer, inadequately studied versions of this chemical.

PBDEs from clothing outgas into the air—and into children's lungs—for as long as one year, despite repeated washings.

Federal regulations, which once required fire retardants on all children's sleepwear, were amended 10 years ago partly in response to concerns about the PBDE exposure. Revised regulations now permit the sale of tight-fitting sleepwear without fire retardants for children under the age of nine months.

Buying clothing, diapers and bedding made from organically grown fibers will avoid all clothing-related toxin exposure for your kids.

See the resource section for children's clothing recommendations.

A NOTE ON DIAPERS

Disposable diapers may be convenient, but they contain polyethylene, dyes and fragrances that can be harmful to your baby.

Some disposables also contain small amounts of dioxin, a well-known carcinogen and endocrine disruptor that is a byproduct of the chlorine bleaching process. Dioxin is also highly toxic to waterways.

Disposable diapers are the third most common item in our landfills. We're throwing away 18 billion of them a year. Five million tons of untreated excrement come into landfills in these diapers and may contribute to groundwater contamination and attract insects that carry and transmit diseases, according to The Center for Biodiversity and Education.

This is a sustainability problem without an easy answer.

A very few parents are buying organic cotton diapers and laundering them twice per use as recommended. This is too cumbersome for most, and consumes energy and water for laundering, but it is the best overall solution if you can possibly manage it.

There are also natural, flushable diaper liners. The best natural disposables I found were gDiapers (www.gdiaper.com), which have an inner lining that you can simply flush down the toilet when soiled. This has the added advantage of no smelly "diaper genie" in the house. Seventh Generation (www.seventhgeneration.com) makes a chlorine-free, dioxin-free disposable diaper that at least keeps these harmful chemicals out of your baby's life. These are a good start, and I remain hopeful that better solutions will be developed in the near future.

Sustainable Step #3:
Find a greener dry cleaner

Find a green dry cleaner in your area to replace traditional dry cleaning and avoid hexane, a highly toxic solvent. Chemicals used in dry cleaning have been shown to cause confusion, sleepiness, and even death with even short-term exposures. Workers in dry cleaning plants are particularly susceptible to these very real problems.

Carbon tetrachloride, trichloroethylene and perchloroethylene (perc) have also been shown to cause liver, kidney and central nervous system effects for people exposed to it in the workplace. These chemicals are a major source of air pollution and they have found their way into municipal water systems.

This problem has an easy fix: Avoid buying clothing that requires dry cleaning.

If you can't avoid dry cleaning entirely, look for a "green" dry cleaner that uses nontoxic and environmentally friendly methods that may include liquid carbon dioxide used in high pressure machines, a silicon-based solvent used in modified traditional dry cleaning machines, or regular water and special detergents in computer-controlled washing machines.

More good news—these greener cleaners are becoming widely available and are now in most major cities. A continuously updated list of dry cleaners across the country that use nontoxic chemicals (and get your clothes just as clean!) is available at www.wellbuilding.com.

Consumer Reports tested these methods in February 2003 and found that the results are comparable to those obtained with "perc"-based traditional dry cleaning without the damage to the health of employees, the environment and ultimately, the consumer.

If none of these methods is available to you and you must use traditional dry cleaning, remove plastic bags from items you bring home from the dry cleaner and hang them in the garage for a few hours before you bring them into the house. This will at least allow a rapid outgassing of the most toxic chemicals.

Sustainable Step #4:
Buy safe personal care products

I've developed a couple of simple solutions to the dilemma of what to put on my skin:

1. Don't put it on your skin if you wouldn't eat it.
2. Don't buy it if you can't pronounce all of the ingredients easily.

Now, of course, I don't expect that you will start snacking on organic shampoo or dining on lavender-scented hand cream. My point is simply to look for products made from natural oils, herbs, vitamins and minerals. If it's easy to pronounce, it is more likely to be safe. Just for fun, try reading the ingredient list from a conventional cosmetic product out loud. If the words don't lightly trip off your tongue, look for something more pronounceable—and safer.

A simple walk through the personal care aisle in a natural foods store or natural supermarket provides a wide selection of aluminum-free deodorants, triclosan-free mouthwashes, fluoride-free toothpastes, natural sunscreens, shampoos, moisturizers and even hair dyes.

The FDA regulates most personal care products as "cosmetics," and that includes anything that can be "rubbed, poured, sprinkled or sprayed on, introduced into or otherwise applied to the human body...for cleansing, beautifying, promoting attractiveness or altering appearance without affecting the body's structure or function."

Our typical cosmetic products are formulated from more than 3,000 ingredients based on petrochemicals or natural animal, vegetable and mineral sources.

There is no mandated requirement for safety testing on these products before they go to market, and the FDA has no power to regulate before there is a known problem. The regulators can only get involved after a product or a particular chemical has been proven to be hazardous.

However, the FDA does have the authority to require complete labeling for all ingredients in these types of products. That's why ingredient disclosure is required on cosmetics labels: so you can make informed choices about the types of chemicals that you put on the porous membrane called your skin.

That all adds up to a caveat: It is your responsibility to know what's in these products and make your choices based on your own knowledge. You can decide what goes onto and into your body.

So that you can make more informed decisions, here is a primer of commonly used dangerous chemicals. Avoid these and you and your family will be healthier.

Phthalates: This tongue-twisting class of petrochemicals is used to make rigid plastics soft and pliable. They're also commonly added to cosmetics and other personal care products. As we have already discussed, phthalates are estrogenic even in minute quantities, and are suspected in a variety of emerging health problems including early puberty, breast cancers, and low sperm counts.

Perfumes, nail polishes, lotions, hairsprays and many other body care products contain phthalates that may also be labeled DBP and DEHP. DBP is used extensively in body care products and DEHP is present in many household products, which we'll address in the next chapter.

A 2000 study conducted by the U.S. Centers for Disease Control and Prevention (CDC) showed that the levels of phthalates in the body tissues of Americans was much higher than previously believed. Researchers found a metabolized form of dibutyl phthalate (DBP) in every single one of the 289 people tested, with highest levels in women of childbearing age (20 to 40). Researchers concluded this was most likely because of the prevalence of cosmetic use in that age group.

DEA and TEA (diethanolamine and triethanolamine): These chemicals can interact with other chemicals in the products, forming carcinogenic nitrosamines. DEA and TEA are often shown on a label as attached to other ingredients, so the label may say "cocamide-DEA" or "TEA-sodium lauryl sulfate."

Formaldehyde: Used as a preservative and often listed as quaternium 15 (which releases formaldehyde). Avoid products that contain any of this toxic chemical that can cause nerve damage, allergies, enhance your sensitivity to other chemicals and even cause cancer.

Bronopol: A pesticide and fungicide often found in bug repellent sticks. It is considered dangerous to humans and its effects include carcinogenicity, reproductive and developmental problems, neurotoxicity and acute toxicity.

Dimethyl dimethyl hydantoin: A microbicide found in a wide range of products from hair conditioners to shampoos, hand soaps, baby wipes and sunscreens, DMDM hydantoin can break down to ingredients that trigger skin sensitivities.

Parabens: Usually combined with other chemicals, parabens have been found in breast tissue samples of women with breast cancer, although no firm link has yet been scientifically established.

Imidazolidinyl urea: Often combined with parabens, this is the most widely used preservative in cosmetics. Classified as a known toxic chemical, the safety of imidazolidinyl urea is under investigation by the National Cancer Institute.

HAIR AND SKIN CARE

You already know that anything you put on your skin, from soap to shampoo, moisturizers to hair dye, deodorant to sunscreen, will be absorbed. Chemicals in these products will be absorbed as well, and they can cause serious health problems. Read labels carefully and be aware that certain types of products tend to be worse than others.

Here are a few of the worst culprits:

Antiperspirants: Virtually all antiperspirants contain aluminum chlorohydrate, the active ingredient that blocks sweat glands and prevents wetness. The research is not yet definitive, but many experts say it is possible that the aluminum in deodorants may also contribute to the buildup of aluminum in the body, since aluminum from other sources has been linked to brain disorders, dementia and Alzheimer's disease. Aerosol sprays, such as antiperspirants, containing aluminum chlorohydrate are often inhaled, potentially worsening the problem. These sprays can also propel aluminum chlorohydrate through the optic nerve right to the brain. Aluminum is one of the few substances than can cross the body's natural defense system, the blood-brain barrier.

A recent definitive study published in the *Journal of Applied Toxicology* by Dr. P. D. Darbre should be the clincher on aluminum-based antiperspirants. This study suggests that aluminum salts in antiperspirants (which she calls "metalloestrogens") create estrogen-like effects in the body and can spur growth of cancer cells in the lab, and calls for further research on the link between antiperspirants and breast cancer.

This is especially worrisome since antiperspirants are applied very near the breast, often onto a shaved armpit. Shaving creates small nicks that can ease the absorption of aluminum near the breast tissue. Antiperspirants are left on the skin all day, increasing time for absorption. This is not an urban legend, but a study published in one of the leading medical journals in the world. So, especially if you are a woman, I recommend dropping the aluminum-based antiperspirants immediately.

Deodorants that are not antiperspirants often contain a bacteria-killing ingredient called triclosan, which has been shown to cause liver damage when it is absorbed though the skin.

Plain baking soda can work very well as a deodorant for some people. The deodorant crystal-stones available in natural food stores are made from crystallized minerals, including alum, a safe mineral, not aluminum.

This is what I use. They're very effective and though they may seem a bit pricey, one $9 stone will last for years.

There are many choices for natural deodorants that look like conventional deodorants but do not contain triclosan or aluminum. Just walk through the natural body care aisle at your local health food store and you will see a wealth of choices.

Sunscreens: Sunscreens and sunblocks have grown from an $18 million annual business in 1972 to over half a billion dollars a year in sales as of this writing. The reason? Sunscreens can protect from UV damage and ultimately skin cancer. Skin cancer is the most common cancer in the United States, with 1.3 million reported cases each year. Although skin cancer incidence is growing at 6 percent a year, because of typical early detection and treatment, it is responsible for only 1 percent of all cancer deaths.

Sunblocks and sunscreens are intended to protect your skin from cancer-causing ultraviolet light. Ironically, this protection from skin cancer exposes our skin to suspected carcinogens, including diethanolamine and related ingredients (DEA, TEA). Other ingredients are suspected endocrine disrupters: benzophenone (oxybenzone), homosalate, octyl-methoxycinnamate (octinoxate), and the parabens (methyl-, ethyl-, butyl-, propyl-).

As you know by now, an "endocrine disrupter" is a chemical that can interfere with the body's hormonal system, which controls growth, metabolism and reproductive fertility among other things. Your hormonal system is not something you want to disrupt. Children are especially vulnerable.

Not only are these chemicals bad for you, they're bad for the environment. Diethanolamine has been found in waterways, posing a threat to animals and humans. Benzophenone has been found in surface water, groundwater, soil and air and may affect the liver and bone marrow of animals ingesting large amounts of contaminated water. These and other endocrine disruptors in sunblocks can also enter the water system when we swim or bathe, eventually winding up in fish, amphibians and marine wildlife, posing a threat to the animals' reproductive cycles.

Your body needs natural sunlight to manufacture vitamin D, a crucial vitamin that has strong protective effects for over a dozen types of cancer. Here are some tips on enjoying the sun without getting burned by potentially toxic sunscreens or the sunburns they are intended to prevent:

- Get some sun every day. Ten to fifteen minutes of unprotected sun on the face and arms is enough to manufacture crucial vitamin D.
- Use safer sunscreens or sunblocks that rely on titanium or zinc oxide to actually scatter the sun's rays before they can burn your skin. Avoid "nano" particles of zinc or titanium, since these ultra-small molecules have unknown effects on the body.
- Keep infants under six months of age out of the sun entirely, and do not risk ANY sunscreen exposure on children of this age.
- Seek the shade between peak sun-strength hours of 10 a.m. and 2 p.m. This is the best time to sit under an awning or umbrella.
- Cover up with an old-fashioned broad-brimmed hat and long-sleeved shirt. Observational research suggests that every one inch of hat brim cuts the odds of skin cancers on the face and neck by 10 percent. I find that lightweight long-sleeved shirts and pants actually keep me cooler in really hot sun.
- Eat your carotenoids. Plants don't have sunscreen. Instead, they manufacture carotenoids, colorful nutrients that protect plants from the harmful effects of the sun. Recent clinical research shows that certain carotenoids, such as astaxanthin, can also protect the skin from sunburn from the inside out. Taken internally, these plant pigments form a protective layer just beneath the skin's surface that offers significant protection from sunburn and UV damage. Other carotenoids, especially lycopene from tomatoes, have exciting applications for internal sun protection as well, and the clinical proof is

building on the power of natural nutrients to protect us from sunburn and sun allergy.

Soap: Many soaps contain petroleum-derived synthetic fragrances, artificial colors and mineral oil that may cause skin rashes and other allergic reactions. I have not been able to use conventional soaps for over a decade, and I certainly don't miss them. There are plenty of natural alternatives available.

Look for vegetable oil-based soaps without artificial fragrances or antimicrobial agents. If you are so inclined, have some fun making your own natural soap from glycerin, essential oils and herbs.

Hero Profile: Aubrey Organics

Aubrey Organics makes the only sunscreen I have been able to find that is safe enough for my family. They have seven different sunscreens that are free of petrochemical additives, carry an unscented version, and do not use "nano" technology in their formulations. Aubrey was founded in 1969 and has deep roots in the organic movement. More at www.aubrey-organics.com.

Shampoos: Even though your hair can't directly absorb toxins that can enter your bloodstream, the thin skin of your scalp can. This is especially important since shampoos and conditioners make their way to the scalp during bathing, when warm water opens the pores, increasing potential for absorption.

Shampoos, conditioners, and other hair care products are commonly made with formaldehyde as a preservative, often labeled quaternium-15. This known carcinogen can also be an irritant to skin, eyes and respiratory passages, even in small amounts. Although the government requires some products containing quaternium-15 to carry a warning label, shampoo is exempted from this requirement.

Many shampoos (and body washes and bubble baths) contain chemicals that look like an alphabet soup: BNPD, TEA and DEA that can combine at random to form carcinogenic nitrosamines. Since nitrosamines are easily absorbed through the skin and your pores are open under hot water, it's best to avoid products containing them.

Dandruff shampoos usually contain selenium sulfide, which can cause vital organs to degenerate if swallowed. Resorcinol, another easily absorbed ingredient in dandruff shampoos, can cause skin and eye irritation, drowsiness, unconsciousness and convulsions. Coal tar is another popular dandruff remedy, with obvious drawbacks. I noticed that my occasional dandruff went away when I started taking omega-3 oils found in cold water fish as a supplement. There is some scientific support to validate my experience.

Hair dyes: An estimated 22 million American women and one in eight American men use some type of hair dye. *Consumer Reports* says 20 chemicals used regularly in hair dyes are potential human carcinogens. These chemicals easily enter the bloodstream because the permanent and semi-permanent dyes are applied at the root of the hair follicle where there is a rich blood supply close to the skin.

Lead, often found in slow-working hair dyes, is a hormone disruptor and carcinogen that is easily absorbed through the skin and accumulates in the bones. One study from Xavier University in Louisiana shows that the amount of lead present in some hair dyes is 10 times the level allowable in paint.

There are more nontoxic and natural hair colorings on the market now than ever before. A stroll down the natural care aisle of your healthy supermarket will yield choices to suit every preference.

Alternately, your kitchen cupboard may contain just what you need. To temporarily enhance dark-colored hair and to cover gray hairs, henna is very effective, as is paprika, beet juice or Red Zinger tea for reddish tones, and ginger, nutmeg or warm coffee for brown tones. Light-colored hair can be highlighted by chamomile, black tea or lemon juice.

Hairspray commonly contains a number of harmful chemicals, including phthalates. Spray products are particularly concerning, since the fine airborne particles in spray lead to absorption directly into the bloodstream through the lungs.

Toothpaste: Most toothpastes include petrochemicals, artificial colors, sweeteners, mineral oil and fluoride. For half a century we have been sold on the idea that fluoride in toothpaste and in our water supply reduces the number of cavities in children and adults. A growing body of scientific evidence shows that there is little cavity protection in fluoride for most people.

We do know that fluoride is toxic at relatively small levels. The EPA limits the amount in drinking water to 4 parts per million, calling it a contaminant over that level. Excessive amounts of fluoride have been proven to cause potentially crippling bone conditions and may cause cancer and nerve damage even at very low levels.

Children have been known to eat toothpaste because it is sweet. The FDA mandates a warning against swallowing the product on all toothpastes containing fluoride—and the warning label says to keep it out of the hands of children under six.

So, replace your paste: Baking soda or a fluoride-free natural toothpaste is a better, safer choice for you and your family.

Mouthwash: Anyone who has ever seen a mouthwash ad knows that it "kills germs by the millions, on contact." That's not good. Those germs are in your mouth and digestive tract for important reasons.

In the mouth, these healthy "bugs" are important for starting the digestive process. In the gut, probiotic bacteria are critical for digestion, nutrient assimilation and immune health. While the bad bacteria may cause tooth decay, faithful flossing and brushing can accomplish the same results.

Mainstream mouthwashes use broad-spectrum antimicrobial agents like triclosan that indiscriminately kill all kinds of bacteria—both bad and good.

Natural minty mouthwashes without antimicrobials are available at your local natural foods store.

Cosmetics

We all want to look our best, and there's nothing wrong with wearing products that enhance our appearance. Just be sure they are safe. Cosmetics are an area where natural choices can make a big difference to your personal health.

Cosmetics are particularly easily absorbed because they are typically put on our most fragile skin and can remain on our bodies for hours at a time.

An FDA study shows some daunting results: 13 percent of the cosmetic preservative butylated hydroxytoluene (BHT) and 49 percent of the carcinogenic pesticide DDT (still found in some lanolin, an ingredient in many cosmetics) is absorbed through the skin.

The government has not mandated wide-scale safety studies of cosmetics, and only 11 percent of the 10,500 ingredients used in cosmetic products have been assessed for safety by the cosmetic industry's review panel. Fully 37 percent of the products tested by the FDA contain chemicals called nitrosamines, which are known carcinogens.

Lipstick is the most toxic cosmetic product, period. It frequently contains several carcinogens, including polyvinylpyrrolidone plastic, saccharin, mineral oil and artificial colors. While there is no hard proof these cause cancer in humans because the studies required would be unethical to conduct, these chemicals do cause cancer in other mammals. Lipstick is particularly dangerous since women actually swallow it by licking their lips, eating or drinking and then reapply it several times in the course of the day. According to a report in *Glamour* magazine, the average woman swallows four to nine pounds of lipstick in her lifetime. That's enough to justify seeking safer alternatives.

Mascara usually contains formaldehyde, alcohol, and plastic resins. These harmful chemicals can get into your eyes and irritate them, then enter your bloodstream though the mucous membranes.

Eye shadow, powdered blush and face powder are all made from talc, a lung irritant that is sometimes contaminated with carcinogenic asbestos.

Perfumes and aftershaves are a soup of chemicals, solvents, and natural essential oils in a base of alcohol, which can include toluene, ketone and other hazardous substances. Approximately 95 percent of the ingredients in perfumes are derived from petrochemicals. In fact, one single scent can have 600 or more chemical ingredients.

Little research has been done on the health effects of scented products, but generally they are recognized as highly allergenic and are notorious for causing skin irritation, headaches, and nausea.

Artificial fragrances are among the first "luxuries" that people with chemical sensitivities have to drop. In all of my conversations over the past decade with people who have made the switch to natural fragrances or stopped using scents altogether, not once have I heard a single person say that they missed them.

You can still look great and protect yourself by using any of the good brands of natural and/or hypoallergenic cosmetics on the market, many of them made from colored clays and natural waxes. Find more information about these alternatives in the resources section.

Hero Profile: Avalon Organics

Avalon Organics makes natural and organic personal care products. Their products are effective at getting your hair and body clean, but they do so without using the nasty chemicals found in conventional products. Avalon has been a leader in this field for years. You can learn more at www.avalonorganics.com.

Sustainable Step #5:
Filter your shower and bath water

It's the end of a long, tiring day and you're looking forward to washing away your troubles with a warm, relaxing shower.

Unfortunately, one nice hot shower in unfiltered tap water exposes you to 50 times the amount of chemicals in a glass of tap water. This is because many of the worst chemicals, including chlorine, vaporize easily in the steam you inhale with every relaxing breath.

Two-thirds of our typical daily total chlorine exposure comes just from showering. People who shower in chlorinated water have a 93 percent higher risk of all types of cancer than those who shower in unchlorinated water, according to a July 2003 report from the U.S. Council of Environmental Quality. That's almost DOUBLE the cancer risk!

An inexpensive carbon filter that attaches just before your showerhead is the simple solution for making showers healthier. It costs about $60 and is a good example of how a small investment can reap big protection for your health. For a list of shower filters and where to buy them, visit www.wellbuilding.com.

Simple Step #6:
Choose natural feminine hygiene

Tampons are made from rayon, a petrochemical-based fiber or cotton, which we already know can contain pesticide residues.

Sanitary napkins and tampons are both often made of fibers bleached with dioxin. Tetrachlorodibenzodioxin (TCDD), one of the toxins found in sanitary napkins and tampons, has been called the most toxic chemical ever produced—and British studies show 130 parts per trillion in tampons and 400 parts per trillion in sanitary napkins. That's a small amount to be sure, but considering that tampons are placed in direct contact with delicate mucous membranes where they are readily absorbed, why take a chance?

Natural unbleached dioxin-free sanitary pads and tampons are available at most natural foods stores, as are washable and reusable organic cotton pads. Tampons labeled "no superabsorbent fibers" are safer.

Seventh Generation, a natural products company that sells a wide range of natural personal care, baby and household products, has just begun production of organic tampons and napkins. You can learn more at www.seventhgeneration.com.

What You Need To Know

- What you put *on* your body is just as important as what you put *in* your body.
- Your skin is the largest organ of your body. It is porous, so what you put on your skin is quickly absorbed into your entire system. Think of your skin more as a sponge rather than as a barrier.
- Clothing made from natural and organic fibers prevents your skin and lungs from being in contact with toxic residues and vapors.
- Disposable diapers are a particular source of toxic waste in our landfills that will take centuries to biodegrade.
- Basic personal care products ranging from soap to toothpaste to shampoo are loaded with potentially dangerous chemicals.
- Chemicals from cosmetics are particularly easily absorbed because they are typically put on our most fragile skin and remain on our bodies for hours.
- Safe and natural alternatives are widely available at almost any health and natural food store.

Part II

Sustainable Home

CHAPTER 4

Sustainability in the Home

"Charity begins at home, but should not end there."
—Thomas Fuller

HOME IS WHERE THE HEART IS. It's also where we spend the vast majority of our time eating, cleaning, sleeping, playing and tinkering in our yards and gardens. For most of us (my family included), a home is the biggest investment we ever make and it's the major expense in our yearly spending budget. Making home a safer and more sustainable place for you and your family is a matter of simple choices that can make a big difference.

Sustainability at home is a critical bridge between personal and environmental sustainability. Seemingly small actions, such as reducing disposables and recycling, can have a tremendous impact on our environment. Our home-related purchases influence business supply chains, extending well beyond the operations of our household. Making your home safer and more sustainable is a matter of making simple choices. Those choices can make a meaningful difference not only for your family's health but also for the environment by reducing waste, chemical use, and reliance on irreplaceable fossil fuels.

Little changes can make a big difference. For example:

- If we all just used a glass instead of a water bottle and a coffee mug instead of a Styrofoam cup, we would save 244 billion bottles and cups made from petrochemical-based plastics from entering the U.S. waste stream each year.

- The average person in the U.S. produces 1,609 pounds of waste each year. Recycling can cut your waste stream by up to 75 percent. If each of us recycled just paper, glass and metal, we would save 162 million tons of material from entering American landfills each year.

- The average suburban lawn uses six times more chemicals per acre than conventional farming. And your kids and pets play on that lawn. If just 10 percent of us switched to natural lawn care, more than half a billion pounds of synthetic fertilizers, pesticides and herbicides would be prevented from entering the environment and our kids' bodies.

- Collectively, we dump 32 million pounds of toxic chemistry down our drains each day, just from household cleaning chemicals. That doesn't count what goes into our indoor air. Switching to green alternatives keeps these chemicals out of our bodies and out of our water supply.

- Energy and fuel efficiency can dramatically reduce use of fossil fuels. Insulating your home can save you up to 15 percent on your utility bills each month.

The tradeoffs don't have to be expensive. For example, natural cleaning products that are just as effective as the conventional products that they replace are now widely available in retail stores. You can even clean almost anything in your house safely, sustainably and inexpensively with vinegar, baking soda, washing soda and/or vegetable-based liquid soap. You can replace toxic pesticides and weed killers for your garden with a few simple ingredients Grandma used to use that will do the work effectively and safely. And, you can even save money by improving the energy efficiency of your home with just a few hours of work.

WHAT YOU CAN DO–
7 Sustainable Steps

1. Conserve by increasing efficiency
2. Recycle
3. Clean green
4. Furnish for health
5. Breathe easier
6. Say "no" to disposables
7. Green your yard

Sustainable Step #1:

Conserve by increasing efficiency

Americans represent less than 5 percent of the world's population, but we consume 40 percent of the global supplies of oil and 23 percent of the natural gas and coal. We have an average of 1.3 people per car—for every man, woman and child in the country. We are simply consuming too much and we can do better.

You don't have to make big sacrifices or spend boatloads of money in order to live a greener life at home. In fact, by adding a few simple, sustainable changes to your lifestyle, you will end up saving money on the household budget's bottom line. That's something we can all appreciate. Here are the top ways you can cut energy consumption in your home:

- **Seal up the cracks:** Closing small cracks around windows, doors and electrical outlets with sealant will go a long way toward tightening up your house and preventing heat or air conditioning from escaping through those cracks. Green architect Bob Swain estimates that if you added up all those cracks, you would find that you had a two-foot-square hole in your house. Imagine how much can escape through a hole that size! Swain estimates you'll save as much as 15 percent of your heating and cooling bill. Look for sealant foams that are not based on petrochemicals, such as AFM Safecoat products, available at www.alerg.com.

- **Turn down the thermostat:** Each two degrees of thermostat change can save up to 8 percent in your monthly heating or cooling bill. Add a sweater in the winter and conserve resources and hard-earned dollars. In summer, open windows in the evening to let in cool air and close windows and drapes on the sunny side of the house in the daytime to help keep the house cooler. When it's possible, use cost-efficient fans for cooling instead of air conditioning. Ceiling fans will circulate cool air in the summer and keep warm air closer to the floor in winter, making your heating and cooling systems more efficient.

- **Replace your light bulbs:** Compact fluorescent light bulbs are four times more efficient than standard incandescent bulbs and they last much longer. Standard bulbs use 95 percent of the energy they consume to produce heat, and only 5 percent for light. A 27-watt compact fluorescent gives off the same light as a standard 100-watt bulb—yet it burns a cool 10,000 hours longer. Compact fluorescents cost anywhere from $2 to $3 apiece, about four times as much as standard light bulbs, but the amount of energy they save over their long lives will more than make up for the difference. Replace your five most frequently used bulbs and save $60 a year in energy costs. Replace standard fluorescent light bulbs with full-spectrum compact fluorescents and save energy while boosting your mood. They're more expensive—about $14 apiece if you buy four or more—but they can save you from the depression some people experience in the winter months, sometimes called seasonal affective disorder (SAD). Experts say if every American household replaced three standard light bulbs with compact fluorescents, the energy savings would be the equivalent of taking 3 million cars off the road.

- **Turn off the lights:** Turning off all lights and computers when not in use is an obvious, easy and painless way to reduce total energy consumption and save on your power bill.

- **Conserve water:** The average American uses 100 gallons of water before leaving the house in the morning, doing things like flushing toilets and leaving water running while brushing teeth. Taking a five-minute shower instead of a bath saves at least 10 gallons of water. Installing a low-water-consumption toilet saves at least two gallons per flush. Doing only full loads of laundry and—this one is a surprise— using your dishwasher instead of hand-washing dishes saves water. A fully loaded dishwasher cuts the water used to do dishes. Using soaker hoses rather than traditional sprinklers, which have a very high evaporation rate, saves water on the lawn and garden.

- **Lose the plastic:** This does not mean throwing out all the plastic things in your house. That would wastefully clog up the landfills. Use your plastic mop buckets and picnic supplies and outdoor chairs, but when it's time to replace anything plastic in your home, consider alternatives: metal buckets, paper plates for picnics, and sustainably harvested wooden outdoor furniture. There are a few places I would recommend getting rid of harmful plastics now: in drinking cups for both children and adults; children's toys, especially where children might chew on them; and vinyl shower curtains. All of these are sources of dangerous chemicals like phthalates. Replace them with ceramic cups for hot liquids, toys made out wood and other traditional materials, and shower curtains made of tightly woven cotton fibers.

- **Buy recycled paper:** If every household in the United States replaced just one box of facial tissue with 100 percent recycled ones, we could save 163,000 trees. If every household in the U.S. just replaced one roll of toilet paper with 100 percent recycled toilet paper, we could save 423,900 trees. If every household in the U.S. replaced just one roll of paper towels with 100 percent recycled ones, we could save 544,000 trees. And if every household in the U.S replaced just one package of paper napkins with 100 percent recycled ones, we could save 1 million trees. Add them all up and we could save more than 2 million trees with these simple changes. Conserving trees has a powerful protective effect on our planetary ecosystem. Think carefully before you buy disposable paper goods. The Natural Resources

Defense Council has a comprehensive listing of specific products and their recycled or post-consumer content at www.nrdc.org. You can find more in the resources section.

- **Look for the Energy Star™ label:** Whenever you're replacing appliances of any type, look for the Energy Star certification that these products are as energy efficient as today's technology allows. Energy Star certification applies to virtually any type of appliance ranging from washers, dryers and refrigerators to telephones, computers and televisions.

Sustainable Step #2:
Recycle

Every man, woman and child in America generates four pounds of trash a day. That's more than 1 billion pounds, every day, 7 days a week, 365 days a year—close to 400 billion pounds a year; 40 percent of that waste is paper and cardboard, 18 percent is yard waste, 9 percent metals and 8 percent plastic and other products.

Where does it all go?

Of these staggering amounts, more than 70 percent of the waste is buried in landfills. We now recycle 27 percent of our trash, a substantial improvement over the past. If we could just increase that to 35 percent, the EPA says our greenhouse gases would be reduced as much as if nearly 7 million cars were taken off the road. Could you recycle 10 percent more of your household trash? That would make the difference.

We can do better. Virtually all municipalities offer recycling now. If you have items that are unusual and your recycling program will not accept them, call your local department of sanitation and ask where you might be able to take them to be recycled.

If you have toxic items to dispose of, including paint, chemicals, pesticides, tires, batteries and the like, ask your department of sanitation what special arrangements need to be made for disposal.

Most tire and auto repair stores will also recycle tires and car batteries for a small fee.

Car batteries as well as the batteries that power your iPod or your cell phone are particularly problematic because they contain mercury and lead that can leach into the ground and into groundwater when they are tossed into landfills.

Most of us get rid of our computers long before they wear out. Computers pose special disposal problems because they contain lead and mercury that can pollute groundwater. The EPA says the U.S. government alone disposes of approximately 10,000 computers a week. Before you throw away a computer, see if a local school, library or thrift shop will take it. You'll also get a tax deduction. They may even help you locate an individual student who needs a computer and can't afford it.

If you need to dispose of any hazardous items like these, ask your local sanitation department what to do with them. If you don't get an answer, you can learn where to safely dispose of these products by calling 1-800-CLEANUP or visiting www.earth911.org.

Most importantly, before you buy any product, from packaged food to computers, consider its recyclability. Factoring potential for recycling into your purchase decision will help create larger markets for sustainable goods.

Sustainable Step #3:
Clean green

Common household chemicals can be hazardous to your health.

And the natural solutions are far more economical.

Why spend big bucks on a wide variety of toxic cleaning materials when a few simple, safe and cheap ingredients will clean virtually anything in your home?

I'm talking about really simple basics: baking soda, white vinegar, lemon juice, borax, vegetable-based liquid soap, and washing soda, plus a few others that most of us already have on hand. Old-fashioned cleaning doesn't require any secret chemical formulas.

Green cleaning is also convenient. It doesn't require any more elbow grease to disinfect a counter top or a toilet with a solution of borax, vinegar and water or to absorb moisture in a damp basement with a bucket of powdered lime. Even cleaning an oven, the most hated of all household tasks, is no more difficult with a natural approach. Simply spray on a mixture of baking soda, water and a few drops of liquid soap, let it sit overnight and wipe clean in the morning.

If that all sounds too rustic for your tastes, consider trying nontoxic cleaners from reputable companies such as Seventh Generation or Ecover, available at your local health or natural foods grocery store. These companies have created effective and convenient versions of the most popular cleaning supplies, but without the dangerous ingredients found in conventional commercial cleaning products.

Not only are conventional commercial cleaning products expensive, many of them are toxic. Remember, these are the same products that you have to lock up to keep young children from touching, yet we often unlock them and then spray them on our countertops where we put our food or in the air that our families breathe!

Laundry products are a major source of water pollution and contain chemicals that can cause health problems, such as skin, lung and eye irritations and allergies. One big culprit is petrochemical-based fragrances used in many of these products. Laundry soap also contains surfactants (which change the surface tension of water) that enter our waterways. Standard bleach contains concentrated chlorine, a broad-spectrum antimicrobial. Dryer sheets can contain chloroform, camphor and ethylacetate, which appear on the EPA's hazardous waste list. Several companies, such as Ecover and Seventh Generation, carry alternative laundry products that get your clothes just as clean without chemical residues and without the environmental negatives.

All purpose cleaners contain chlorinated phosphates, complex phosphates, dry bleach, kerosene, petroleum-based surfactants, sodium bromide, glycol ether, Stoddard solvent, EDTA and naphtha. All of these are bad for you.

Chlorinated products can form dangerous organochlorine compounds, which are stored in human fat cells and can enter breast milk. Morpholine is toxic to the liver and kidneys. Other cleaning compounds are toxic to the central nervous system and can cause headaches, brain fog and even mental illness.

Common cleaning chemicals are extremely toxic to the environment and some must be handled as hazardous waste. Phosphates can cause waterways to become clogged with algae and can also bind with other compounds, such as DDT, to form even more hazardous materials. EDTA can lead to heavy metal contamination of waterways, while petrochemicals from cleaning products break down slowly in the environment and contaminate air and water.

Glass cleaners can contain several types of solvents, phosphates, ammonia, petroleum-based waxes, phosphoric acid, alkyl phenoxy ethanols, naphtha and butyl cellusolve.

Several of these are central nervous system depressants and organic solvents that often contain contaminants like benzene, which has been shown to cause cancer. Butyl cellusolve is found in many glass cleaners and is particularly dangerous to humans.

Hand dishwashing detergents may be loaded with toxic petroleum-based surfactants, naphtha, chloro-o-phenylphenol, diethanolamine complex phosphates and sodium nitrates.

Chloro-o-phenylphenol is a metabolic stimulant, while diethanolamine is a possible liver poison. Naphtha is a neurotoxin that can cause serious mental malfunctions. Both are considered hazardous waste, and other substances in these products break down slowly in the environment and contaminate air and water.

Disinfectants and antibacterials are made from dangerous chemicals like naphtha, butyl cellusolve and petroleum-based surfactants. The chlorinated germicides in these products pose an even greater problem because they kill most or all bacteria in the environment where they are being used. Breeding new strains of resistant bacteria while wiping out beneficial bacteria is not a good idea in terms of human health or the planet's health. Some experts say our obsession with disinfecting our homes and killing bacteria may ultimately result in lowered immune responses because we won't have everyday exposure to all kinds of bacteria, so we'll become unable to fight off the really bad guys.

I highly recommend a serious housecleaning—starting with what's under your sink and in your cleaning cupboard. Replace them with more environmentally friendly alternatives from your natural foods store.

Hero Profile: Seventh Generation

Seventh Generation is the leading brand of nontoxic cleaning supplies in the U.S. and its products avoid the hazardous ingredients mentioned above. They are the best company I have found for green cleaning products and natural personal care (and they have recently branched out into natural feminine hygiene). Their founder, Jeffrey Hollender, is an author on the topic of corporate sustainability and a pioneer in the field. Learn more about this fantastic company at www.seventhgeneration.com.

Sustainable Step #4:
Furnish for health

The furniture around you may be having a profound effect on your health. It may seem innocuous, but the gases coming from many types of furniture, ranging from mattresses to sofas and even the desk where you work, may be making you sick.

Most of us live indoors for a vast majority of the day. We travel from a house or apartment to a sealed office building and back home without giving it a thought. Did you know that according to the EPA your indoor environment may be as much as five times more polluted than the air outside? That's because furniture and carpets are leaching gases into the air. Your mattress has been treated with flame retardant chemicals. The walls are colored with paints that release toxic chemicals. Paneling and bookshelves and other goods made from particle board release toxins from glues and formaldehyde.

Let me tell you about my friend Daliya Robson, who has a powerful story about the effects common household furnishings had on her health.

Daliya's Story

In 1992, Daliya Robson was a realtor at Century 21 in Capitola, California. She spent a lot of time showing new homes. She noticed that she often felt her eyes and skin were burning. She started to get allergies and headaches, and often felt dizzy and disoriented.

Daliya consulted doctors, who recognized that her symptoms were similar to complaints from people who had inhaled solvents, toxic carpet and paint fumes, pesticide residues, or mold fumes. The doctors reasoned that Daliya had accumulated toxic exposures throughout her life, and at 56 had reached a limit in what she could tolerate. This intolerance was now being aggravated by intense solvent exposures as a byproduct of her job showing homes. She was, in essence, being poisoned each time she showed a house with a fresh coat of paint, a recent administering of pesticides or insecticides, new sealants, new carpets, and brand-new air fresheners.

Daliya retired from real estate and removed all chemical exposures from her life. Feeling better a year later, she established the Nontoxic Hotline, a helpline to warn people about ill effects

continued on the next page

Daliya's Story continued

from toxic surroundings. Most of the people seeking her help line were already ill, since healthy people were blissfully unaware of the dangers in their everyday surroundings. Searching for healthier solutions for her customers led Daliya to develop Nirvana Safe Haven, an online retailer of healthy products designed to help people live safely.

"More and more people are suffering from environmental injury and becoming unable to live a meaningful life," says Daliya. "They're suffering intensely from allergies, asthma and undiagnosed symptoms when they sleep on an old mattress, or buy a new bed full of chemicals, or remodel their bedroom with new carpet."

Common symptoms include a runny nose, burning eyes, depression, impotence, aches and pains, bed wetting, panic attacks, and general malaise. "These do not happen when they sleep on a pure organic cotton and wool mattress or even a 100 percent latex rubber mattress that has been quilted with two or more inches of wool around the top and bottom and covered with organic cotton," says Robson. "And while we cannot prove how many brain cells are destroyed by a toxic mattress for an infant, we are sure the baby will develop better without chemical fumes," she adds.

Organic sleeping materials, such as pure organic wool, can often go further than preventing the onset of unwanted ill effects: "They can help heal people with body pains and provide warmth and comfort for the healthy," she says.

Credit goes to Daliya for helping me with my own chemical sensitivities. You can read more of Daliya's story and learn more about the nontoxic products she has developed at www.nontoxic.com.

REPLACE FURNITURE THAT HAS GAS

Some of your furniture has gas. Replacing that furniture is one of the most important things you can do for your health. Most of today's furniture uses pressboard for its internal structure. Pressboard leaches formaldehyde-containing gas into the air as the glues that it is made from decompose over time. I recommend disposing of all of the pressboard-based furniture that you can do without. When buying furniture, choose sustainably grown solid wood, glass or metal furniture. If you can't replace offgassing furniture, at least remove it from the bedroom where you spend the most time. When it comes to formaldehyde, less is more and none is best.

Chances are good that your furniture contains foam that also off-gasses chemicals into your home. Pillows and padding on upholstered chairs and sofas are usually made from polyurethane foam plastic and are covered with plastic covers. Most upholstery fabrics are synthetic and they are coated with a formaldehyde-based resin to resist stains. One study shows that adding furniture to an empty room tripled the room's formaldehyde levels.

Home furnishings that are safe to use can be found through furniture dealers, decorators and online retailers. As a general rule, solid furniture is safer, and furniture that is more than 50 years old is almost always free from any offgassing chemicals.

When you're buying new wood products, look for the SmartWood or Green Cross labels, which indicate that the wood comes from a sustainably managed forest. For a list of companies that sell non-offgassing furniture, see www.wellbuilding.com.

THE RIGHT PAINT

Common household paints carry warning labels describing what to do in case of overexposure to fumes. All paint is made from resins to help them stick to the surface you intend to cover, pigments for color, and additives to enhance paint performance. Solvents, the largest percentage of the contents of paints by volume, are included to help paint spread and dry evenly.

The most hazardous ingredients in modern paints are called VOCs—volatile organic compounds—which originate in the solvents. These are found primarily in oil-based paints, but they are present in smaller amounts in water-based paints as well. VOCs can affect your central nervous system, cause dizziness and headaches, breathing difficulties, vomiting and other unpleasant symptoms. You might be able to live with this in the short term if you keep windows open right after painting, but research suggests VOCs continue to outgas from painted walls for years.

In addition, VOCs in exterior paints are a major contributor to air pollution. The California Air Resources Board estimates that 100 million pounds of VOCs are released into the air annually by paints and finishes, despite Southern California's strict regulations on paints. The EPA estimates that 11 billion pounds of VOCs are outgassed nationwide each year from exterior paints and coatings.

Reducing exposure to VOCs is relatively easy and inexpensive. When it's time to paint your house, inside or out, choose a water-based paint. Many major manufacturers now have low- or no-VOC paints, so look for this designation on the label. You can find low-VOC paints in paint stores, home improvement stores and online.

For wood finishes, look for water-based finishes labeled "low-odor," "water cleanup" or "two-hour dry," since these versions tend to be much lower in VOC content.

REPLACE OR REMOVE YOUR CARPETS

Most carpets on the commercial market are made of synthetic fibers. These carpets have many of the same problems as furniture. Carpets can emit as many as 120 hazardous chemicals, including neurotoxic solvents like toluene and xylene, and benzene, a potent carcinogen. Padding and carpet backings have even more hazardous chemicals, including pentachlorophenol, and they're often treated with chemical mothproofing, soil repellents, and moisture repellents. Worse yet, carpet is frequently installed over a particle board subfloor that can outgas formaldehyde for years.

The environmental impact of these synthetic materials can be enormous. Most of these fabrics take decades to biodegrade in landfills, since they are primarily made of petrochemical-based or plastic components.

Once installed, carpets can outgas these chemicals over a large surface area. In addition, carpets trap dust, molds and phthalate particles outgassed from plastics in your home.

I recommend removing synthetic carpets if you can and replacing them with bare hardwood floors, perhaps covered by natural cotton or wool area rugs. If you have particle board subflooring, consider removing it or sealing it so it can no longer outgas. The sealer I use is Crystal Air, available at www.nontoxic.com. There are also some very beautiful wool carpets that carry a green label, certified by the Carpet and Rug Institute to be free of toxic chemicals.

Window coverings have many of the same problems as carpets, so choose natural-fiber drapes, curtains and blinds or wood shutters.

AT THE OFFICE

If you work outside your home, you probably spend more time in your office than anywhere else. While you may not be able to change the carpet and cubicles at work, you can offer your input if an office remodel or move is being considered. At the very least, you may be able to convince your company to increase airflow or allow windows to be opened so that built-up fumes can be ventilated out of the space. Even cleaning an existing ventilation system can reap substantial improvement in indoor air quality.

Many companies are increasingly open to making smaller changes: recycling paper, batteries and cell phones; avoiding Styrofoam cups in the break room; using integrated (natural) pest management and using natural air freshener sprays in the bathrooms.

A little bit can make a big difference. Just by making some changes, like recycling more paper in the office, we are saving more than 1,000 trees per year at Garden of Life. We are also recycling batteries and cell phones, keeping their metals out of landfills and the environment.

I created the website www.wellbuilding.com to help people with chemical sensitivities, also called "sick building syndrome," connect with resources that could help them rebuild their wellness. It contains links to resources and other websites organized by topic, from building personal health to green design to creating healthier interiors. We will keep it current as new resources are discovered, and I invite you to visit this site from time to time to get the latest information.

Sustainable Step #5:
Breathe easier

The EPA says indoor air pollution is the nation's number one environmental health problem. They estimate that indoor air is two to five times more polluted than outdoor air, on the average. Since we spend 90 percent of our time inside our homes and offices (and cars, which often outgas chemicals just like furniture), and our homes are increasingly well sealed for energy efficiency, poor interior air quality is a serious problem.

Some types of indoor air pollution are easily recognizable, especially if bad odors, mustiness, mold or mildew are evident.

However, there are other serious problems that may not be so apparent. If you find that you feel noticeably healthier outside of your home, it is likely that you have an indoor air pollution issue. If you or your family members have health problems after new furniture has been brought in or weatherproofing applied or a remodeling project has been completed, indoor air pollution is a probable culprit.

Here are a few simple ways to reduce indoor pollution in your home:
- **Ventilation and air filtration** are the dual answers to many indoor air pollution problems. Your personal fix can be as simple as opening a

few windows on warm days or as complex as a meticulous mold-removal project.

- **Filters:** Putting an activated carbon air filter system in your most occupied rooms will also help clean your air. These filters absorb gases and pollutants that other, more high-tech filters miss. For a list of filters and air purification systems that I think are suitable for home use, see the resource guide. Be sure to clean the filters on a regular schedule.

- **Fans:** Window fans and whole house fans are also very helpful in getting stale air out of your home. Newer models of attic fans operate very quietly as they bring in cool night air and evacuate stale daytime air from your home. They also make cooling more energy efficient.

- **Cleansing houseplants:** You can cleanse your indoor air quite simply by using houseplants. NASA tests show that common houseplants remove toxins through the natural process of photosynthesis—as they take up carbon dioxide, they also pick up airborne pollutants through their leaves. Aloe vera, elephant ear philodendron, ficus and golden pothos are very effective at removing formaldehyde; English ivy, peace lily and corn plants can eliminate most benzene and golden pothos and spider plants are very effective at removing carbon monoxide. See the resources section for more information on plants to help clean house.

- **Control radon gas:** Radon is an odorless, colorless, radioactive gas that occurs naturally when uranium in the soil or bedrock breaks down. Radon is the second most prevalent cause of lung cancer (after smoking) in the United States. A simple and inexpensive test ($15 to $30) can determine if you have radon gas in your home. If you do, it can be easily resolved by the installation of a radon-specific ventilation system that costs between $500 and $2,500 to install.

- **Use a high-efficiency particulate air (HEPA) vacuum:** These types of vacuums capture and contain the smallest particles of contaminated dust on floors and household surfaces. Vacuuming floors and uphol-stered surfaces at least once a week helps to avoid dust buildup, as does vacuuming curtains and drapes frequently. Keeping your home's walk-ways and entrances swept, and using a simple doormat at the entrance, keeps dust from being tracked into the house in the first place.

Sustainable Step #6:
Say "no" to disposables

Let's admit it: Disposables make our lives easier. However, given the limitations of our overflowing landfills, the need to rethink disposable products, designed from the beginning to be tossed, is increasingly evident.

"Disposable" is a literally a dirty word.

The environmental advocacy group Envirowise estimates that 80 per-cent of the products we use are discarded after a single use.

Everywhere you turn there are disposable razors, cups, plates, utensils, food packaging, paper goods, grocery bags, dust cloths, mop heads, even toilet brushes. We live in a disposable society. Even computers and cars could be considered disposable—at least many of us treat them that way. As soon as a newer, better, faster or sexier model comes along, we dump the current model.

Worse yet, many of the products we toss after one single use are made of plastic. Since these take hundreds of years to biodegrade, they are unnecessarily clogging our landfills and even our oceans.

Here are the top "disposables" that can most easily be replaced with convenient alternatives:

Disposable grocery bags: Since their introduction in the 1970s, han-dled plastic carry bags have become the world's favorite way to carry pur-chases. They're light, cheap, strong, waterproof and durable. For these reasons, we use as many as a trillion each year. Most are trashed, a tiny fraction are recycled and a good many are littered or break free of waste bins and become eyesores that kill fish, birds and other wildlife. Most wind up in landfills where they hang around for a thousand or more years.

Nearly 80 percent of the plastic trash in the U.S. comes from bags and packaging and only 3.2 percent is recycled.

Some municipalities are considering levying taxes on the bags. Many stores offer recycling of shopping bags and most supermarkets offer paper bags as an alternative. Many natural foods stores will credit your purchase if you bring back their bags to be reused, or provide you with a small rebate if you don't use a bag. If you really want to do it right, reusable cloth bags are the best way to avoid being a consumer of disposable shopping bags.

Disposable cups used for coffee and other drinks: What's so hard about carrying your own ceramic mug to work or keeping a stainless steel travel cup in your car? Many merchants are actually charging less for customers who use their own cups, since it cuts their expenditures on disposable cups. This is a great example of how everyone can win when we keep the welfare of the environment in our minds.

Disposable chopsticks: Disposable chopsticks are a classic example of waste. Trees cut for these one-time-use products have decimated forests in Asia and caused widespread environmental devastation, ranging from mudslides to siltation, which has killed coral reefs and wiped out once-teeming fishing grounds. If you want to use chopsticks, buy a washable

Hero Profile: NatureWorks

NatureWorks makes a new kind of environmentally friendly plastic from corn. This division of Cargill is processing corn into a form of plastic called PLA that can be made into food containers, disposable cups, and other common applications for which petroleum-based plastic would normally be used. The NatureWorks corn-plastic takes less energy to make, uses a renewable resource as raw material, and can be composted after use. Learn more at www.natureworks.com.

pair and carry them with you. You can also just give it up and use a fork that can be washed.

Disposable batteries: Almost everything runs on batteries, and you never seem to think about them until they run out. Batteries are a leading source of heavy metal contamination in our landfills. Lead and cadmium eventually make it to your groundwater. Rechargeable batteries are an easy and more convenient choice, and one you are already using in important gadgets such as cell phones. Forward-thinking companies have even created solar chargers for batteries, which can generate totally clean energy for your electronic devices. I bought my Brunton solar cell phone charger at www.rei.com.

Applying a green filter to your purchase decisions can help you pass up the disposables when there are more durable alternatives available.

Simple Step #7:
Green your yard

Natural and organic gardening and lawn care will go a long way toward keeping your home environment and our planet healthy.

Over the long term, natural means of pest and weed control are more effective than synthetics, since strong plants produce their own pest and weed control. In conventional gardening, pests can build up a tolerance to pesticides over time and then come back with a vengeance.

Today, the typical suburban homeowner uses six times the pesticides and synthetic fertilizers per acre as a conventional (non-organic) farmer, according to The Organic Center. We are applying a witches' brew of weed and pest control products, fertilizers, cleansers, stains and who-knows-what to keep those manicured lawns and precise gardens. The National Academy of Sciences says, "Suburban gardens and lawns receive heavier pesticide applications than most any other land area in the United States" including agricultural land. In fact, the United States consumes more than one-third of all pesticides used in the world.

Lawns are unnatural by their very design because they are composed of non-native grasses fertilized and stimulated into hypergrowth, then cut short weekly. In my household, we use natural lawn care, including natural fertilizers and hand-pulling of weeds rather than spraying. Our lawn grows a bit more slowly than the neighbors' and isn't a perfect golfing green, but we think that it is more beautiful to see our girls playing out there and know they are safe.

Pesticides are closely regulated by the U.S. government, but that doesn't imply that they are safe to walk on barefoot. Pesticides and herbicides are contaminating our soil, air and water—and ourselves.

An old study from the National Cancer Institute still hasn't been refuted nearly 20 years after it was completed. The 1987 NCI study concluded that children who lived in households where outdoor pesticides were regularly used were six to nine times more likely to develop leukemia and, when indoor pesticides were used, the figure increased fourfold.

Pesticide poisoning is the second most common cause of household poisoning in the U.S., resulting in 2.5 million poisonings annually by products as common as ant and roach killer, fly sprays and insect repellents.

Of the 1,400 active pesticide ingredients available on the market today, more than 100 are known to cause cancer. Among the worst offenders are chlorpyrifos, diazinon, the herbicides 2,-4-d and banvel, and the fungicides benomyl and daconil.

That green on most suburban lawns is deceiving. Did you know that just using a power mower to mow your lawn will emit more

Hero Profile: Gardens Alive!

Gardens Alive! is a company focused on natural and organic lawn and garden care. On the company's website, www.gardensalive.com, you can find an organic version of anything you need to maintain those beautiful lawns and gardens.

exhaust in half an hour than a car driven 187 miles? The EPA says 20 percent of all air pollution is caused by power equipment used for lawns and gardens.

If you must have that silky green lawn and flower beds worthy of an English mansion, there are plenty of natural products that can give you similar results without the negative environmental impact.

Organic gardens: Organic gardening can be immensely rewarding. Working the soil, seeing seeds grow into plants, moving your body outside and enjoying the harvest restore a connection to nature and to our food supply that is often missing from our high-tech lives. We have a small organic garden in raised beds in our backyard, and nothing tastes better than a strawberry from that garden.

You might consider converting part of your lawn into a wildflower meadow or an organic herb garden. Even the smallest organic garden—a potted tomato on the balcony or even a jar full of alfalfa sprouts on the kitchen windowsill—can make a difference to your health and reduce the chemical load on the planet.

Pests can be contained with companion planting, by planting crops that insect and animal predators find repugnant, by introducing beneficial insects that prey upon pests, and with natural mineral and botanical pest control.

Weeds can be controlled by the type of bed you create (raised beds tend to have fewer weeds), the type and amount of mulch you apply and by hand-weeding. For more on organic gardening, see the resources section.

CHAPTER 5

Sustainable Building and Retrofitting

"They paved paradise, put up a parking lot."
—Joni Mitchell

WHEN MY FAMILY MOVED to Florida, we decided to make our home as sustainable as practical, from the design and layout to the "green" building materials. After an aggressive refurnishing of our older home in Pennsylvania several years earlier, here was our chance to start from scratch and really do it right. We were already friends with Bob Swain, a leading architect in the "green building" movement. We considered issues like size, siting, building materials, ventilation, insulation, and energy efficiency. We carefully examined everything from concrete treatments to long overhangs to the pool water filtration system that added up to a sustainable home. Our home ended up being a dream come true. It was also one of the most intensive learning experiences of our lives.

One important learning was that many of the "green" elements of our construction could easily be incorporated into a remodel. Some, like the filters we applied to our water and air system or the saline pool which uses one-sixth the level of chlorine as a conventional pool, can easily be retrofitted to an existing home. We learned that you don't have to build a new home to live green, and that smarts count for a lot more than money.

We've been extremely fortunate to be able build a "green" dream home, and I realize that not everyone can. The good news is that you don't have to build a new home to engage in sustainable living—so don't send your home to a landfill! In fact, the best path may actually be quite the opposite: to take your existing home and make it as environmentally friendly and healthy as possible.

New construction, no matter how environmentally friendly, requires the use of new materials, further depleting the earth's resources and putting more construction waste into landfills. Building and construction materials worldwide consume 3 billion tons of raw materials or 40 percent of global use, according to David Roodman and Nicholas Lenssen, authors of *A Building Revolution: How Ecology and Health Concerns are Transforming Construction*.

Roodman and Lenssen found that:

- 55 percent of the wood cut for non-fuel uses is for construction;
- 40 percent of the world's materials and energy is used by buildings; and
- 30 percent of newly-built or renovated buildings suffer from "sick building syndrome," exposing occupants to stale or mold- and chemical-laden air.

What's more, Oikos, a green building organization for contractors, says 40 to 50 percent of job site waste is wood—3,000 pounds for a typical 2,000-square-foot house—and drywall waste makes up another 15 percent, or 2,000 pounds. These products can often be recycled and reused if your contractor is agreeable. Wood can be turned into mulch right on the job site and drywall waste can be cut into small pieces and used to enhance insulation value in attics and basements.

WHAT YOU CAN DO—
4 Sustainable Steps

1. Insulate for efficiency
2. Use sustainable and healthy building materials
3. Think power-fully
4. Heal your home

Sustainable Step #1:
Insulate for efficiency

Green architect Bob Swain says closing out the elements can be simple and inexpensive. Depending on where you live, these elements may be heat, cold, wind or water. Usually you'll have more than one challenge. In some climates, you may have to deal with all four.

Make Mother Nature your friend

Swain, who has spent the past 30 years masterminding green design projects ranging from residences and spas to an environmentally conscious city larger than Miami Beach now being constructed on the coast of China, recommends knowing your site well.

Your landscaping can yield significant home energy savings. First, Swain recommends familiarizing yourself with your home's micro-climate, sun orientation and prevailing winds. That's because insulation starts outside your house. For example, you might plant a row of trees to block cold winds and dramatically improve your heat conservation. Sometimes simply planting a tree in a strategic location can be the solution for too much heat coming through your windows in summer. Simply installing shades to block summer sun will help keep your living space cooler naturally, says Swain. Conversely, leaving shades open in winter brings in maximum amounts of warming sunlight.

"Little things like that can make a big difference in your cooling bill," he says. Another cooling solution: Open more windows on the cooler north side of the house and fewer on the warmer south side. For a warmer house in winter, close off unused rooms. A heavy curtain across a stairway can keep valuable warm air from rising to upper rooms, which are typically used less.

The biggest bang for your buck

An investment of under $100 for a programmable thermostat can save you 20 percent or more on energy consumption for both heating and cooling. This may be one of the best small investments you can make in retrofitting your existing home because it minimizes energy usage in rooms where heating or cooling is not needed and economizes at times when you are not home.

Programmable thermostats automatically adjust your home's temperature settings, allowing you to save energy while you're away or sleeping. Look for a programmable thermostat bearing the EngeryStar™ label. These thermostats are mercury-free, and available at most home improvement stores.

FANS, AWNINGS AND BETTER WINDOWS

Awnings or covered porches can reduce your cooling bills and extend your outdoor enjoyment. Even in hot south Florida, we enjoy the shade of our long covered porch 52 weeks per year. And the house stays cooler because the windows are shaded even when the sun is at its strongest.

Whole house fans that run quietly and efficiently at night can draw in cool air and substantially lower your cooling bill. A whole house fan is about one-eighth the operating costs of an air conditioning system. This means that even if you're just supplementing your air conditioning with a fan that brings in cool night air, you'll be lowering your energy bills and saving natural resources.

In cooler climates, the installation of storm windows is an investment that will return substantial energy conservation for a minimal outlay. This one-time expense in energy efficiency typically pays back the cost of installation within four years.

If you're planning an addition or if you have need for new windows, consider double- or even triple-pane windows for increased energy efficiency. Wood- or metal-frame windows with a thermal barrier are an energy-efficient, sound choice.

If you are designing the house from scratch, careful placement of windows to maximize protection from the sun in warm climates or bringing in as much sunlight as possible in colder climates can make a substantial difference in heating and cooling efficiency.

Sustainable Step #2:
Use sustainable and healthy building materials

Whether you're replacing the floor in a small bathroom, adding a room or building an entire new home, the building material you use will have a profound effect on your health and the health of our environment.

Fortunately, many new and more sustainable building products have come on the market in recent years.

Your solution may be as simple as choosing ceramic tile or natural stone flooring to replace vinyl and/or carpet that outgasses.

Kitchen cabinets are a major source of indoor air pollution. Choosing solid wood cabinetry instead of cabinets made of formaldehyde-laden pressboard or particle board will prevent indoor air pollution through outgassing. It is important to have the cabinet base structures (boxes) constructed from safe materials, not just the cabinet doors.

For the structure of the cabinets in my own home renovation, I used Sierra Pine's medium-density fiberboard, Medex (see www.wellbuilding.com for the latest). This is a safe pressboard made from non-offgassing materials. Medex is used in the construction of museum displays, because delicate documents and artifacts can't take offgassing either! You may be surprised to find the cost of natural and nontoxic materials is not much different from conventional products.

Take plenty of time to decide what you need and how to accomplish it. Contractors frequently remark that homeowners' eyes are bigger than their pocketbooks and clients often discover they don't need as much space as they thought they did. A good architect or contractor can help you sketch out your addition. If you've decided on a really major remodel or new construction, it's probably wise to bring an architect into the picture. Most building codes require an architect's signature on any major building plans.

If you are hiring a contractor, whether it's for a large or small project, be sure that you are in agreement about the types of materials that will be used, including all types of adhesives, which can have an exceptionally high degree of toxicity. Sit down with your contractor and go through the entire list of products that will be used, including brand names. If any of them are objectionable to you, it is your right to specify alternatives. You may be surprised to find that many builders have become much more conscious of sustainable and nontoxic steps throughout the entire building process.

The six things you can do now to "green" your new home or remodel:

1. Know the climate, weather patterns and sun orientation.
2. Keep out carpet to reduce dust and molds.
3. Be efficient with layout.
4. Think small and don't overbuild.
5. Use sustainable materials.
6. Incorporate ventilation into the design to reduce dust mold, for energy efficiency and easier cooling.

Some other things to consider about major additions or new structures that will help make them more sustainable:

• Open floor plans require fewer walls, thereby cutting down on material costs and making a smaller space seem larger.

• An efficient layout can save on materials. For example, if you will have two bathrooms and they are one above the other, your piping needs will be reduced.

• Symmetrical designs save on labor costs.

• Prefabricated systems, especially wall systems, save costs. There are new moveable walls that can allow for a family's changing needs.

• It's a good idea to visit your site frequently and keep a close watch on the materials being used.

ALTERNATIVE BUILDING MATERIALS

Over the years, a wide variety of alternative building materials have emerged, each with its beauties and each with its drawbacks.

If you're undertaking a construction project, look for a local green builder who can help you incorporate sustainably harvested materials and other natural materials into your plan.

I'm not going to spend a lot of time explaining what's available, because every construction project is different. Here is a list for you to consider and discuss with a contractor:

- Concrete in many forms
- Modular construction
- Mortarless blocks
- Straw bale with a cement stucco skin
- Earth bermed (structure built partially below ground for extra insulating capacity)
- Rammed earth
- Used and recycled materials from other construction projects and from houses or buildings that have been demolished

Here is a list of the most unhealthy substances used in any type of construction and suggestions for reducing or eliminating toxicity:

Adhesives: These are arguably the most toxic and environmentally damaging substances used in conventional building. They are used for everything from gluing wood pieces together to affixing flooring materials to underlayment. The underlayments themselves are frequently made of composite boards laden with glues and formaldehyde. Adhesives can contain everything from formaldehyde to compounded petroleum distillates like hexane, benzene, toluene, naphthalene and others that can cause nausea, dizziness, drowsiness, headaches and central nervous system damage. *Sustainable alternatives:* Water-based adhesives will do virtually every job equally well with less cleanup time. Certain solutions are even simpler: Wood flooring can be nailed down and tile can be installed with mortar.

Joint compound: Premixed joint compound used on sheetrocked walls contains highly toxic vinyl acetate polymer, which outgasses over a long period of time, and acetaldehyde, a solvent that outgasses fairly rapidly. Texturized popcorn-type ceilings are no longer fashionable, but resist any urge to install them because the spray-on type may contain chemicals that, under California law, must be labeled as "known to be carcinogenic." If you want a textured wall finish, ask for help in your local home supply store, choose a low-VOC paint and add texturizing substances, including sand. *Sustainable alternatives:* Dry joint compound powder that is mixed with water and contains no toxic chemicals.

Grout sealer: Used to seal the spaces between ceramic tiles, these sealers usually include petroleum-based chemicals. Any tile can be installed with mortar and grout, which are nontoxic. Some products recommend latex sealers, which outgas least quickly. There are also water-based grout sealers on the market.

Caulk: These sealing compounds are made of acrylic, latex and/or silicone, depending on their purpose. They are almost invariably compounded with mineral spirits, toxic solvents that are made of any of a number of petroleum-based solvents. They can cause many of the same symptoms as those caused by adhesives. *Sustainable alternatives:* Caulks that contain no mineral spirits.

Plumbing pipes: Polyvinyl chloride or PVC pipe, used in the vast majority of American houses, is a hard plastic that leaches almost nothing into the water that travels through it. However, the adhesives that hold pipes together can outgas and potentially be as toxic as adhesives and other solvents. Clearly, the manufacture of PVC is harmful to the environment and it lives forever in landfills if you decide to remove it. *Sustainable alternatives:* Copper piping or PVC piping using connectors to minimize use of adhesives.

Insulation and sheathing: Much of the insulation used in today's construction is formaldehyde-urea foam, which was banned for years due to health concerns, only to be un-banned some years later by the courts. The Consumer Product Safety Commission continues to warn consumers of "substantial risk" of respiratory, eye and throat irritation, dizziness and nausea that can become serious with prolonged exposure. Rigid polystyrene, a medium-soft plastic, can cause similar problems in people with sensitivities. Plywood sheathing contains toxic glues that can outgas for decades. *Sustainable alternatives:* My favorite insulating material is Icynene, an advanced foam that is sprayed directly on to the underside of roofs in the attic space. Icynene is healthier because it has zero offgassing and is not a substrate for mold or fungus. Icynene also provides sound insulation, important for homes like mine that have steel roofs. More at www.icynene.com. Fiberglass insulation is a bit tricky to handle in installation, and it contains a small amount of formaldehyde, but it is generally safe after it is installed. There are numerous types of cellulose insulation, including a blown-in type that is made from recycled newspapers. Other alternatives: wool batts, cementitious magnesium oxide foam, structural insulated panels, vermiculite and perlite. Check to see if any of these are manufactured close to your home and make your choices with energy expenditures on transportation in mind.

Sustainable Step #3:
Think power-fully

I'll be going into renewable energy sources at much greater length in Chapter Six, but renewable power sources for your existing home or for new construction are worth mentioning here in brief.

Solar: Photovoltaic technology has progressed to the point where nearly any home can meet its hot water needs with a solar panel or two on the roof. The U.S. Department of Energy says a typical solar water-heating system reduces the need for conventional water heating by about two-thirds. This free power minimizes the expense of electricity or fossil fuel to heat the water and reduces the associated environmental impact. Solar-powered attic fans and even solar home alarm systems are becoming common because they are viable and cost-efficient ways of reducing your power consumption. If you want to find a contractor in your area who can install solar products, visit www.findsolar.com.

Wind: Residential wind turbines are expensive ($6,000 to $22,000, depending on the system you choose), but they are efficient enough to save up to 90 percent on your power bill when they are running, according to the American Wind Energy Association. These residential-scale wind turbines are designed to begin generating power at wind speeds of 7 to 10 miles per hour, which is available in many areas of the country. Larger-scale wind energy requires large towers that are unacceptable for urban or even most suburban communities. One of the beauties of wind energy is that federal regulations require utilities to connect with and purchase power from small wind energy systems. You can learn more about buying and finding a contractor to install alternative home wind turbines and other home power generation appliances at www.utilityfree.com.

Hydropower: Water power is probably the cheapest and most reliable alternative energy source, but home generation is very limited unless you happen to be located in precisely the right place, near a stream or river, and with sufficient drop for the water to turn the turbine and generate power. For a small water turbine to power the average household, you'll need at least three feet of fall and at least 20 gallons per minute of flow. Home hydropower is a wonderful, clean and cheap solution for a small number of people.

While there are people who live entirely off the grid, that is difficult and not at all practical for most of us. Most systems require at least one alternative energy source to avoid major inconveniences when there are several cloudy or wind-still days in a row. The battery banks required to store energy are expensive, often impractical and have their own environmental problems because they eventually have to be disposed of in landfills. Most users of alternative energy now are connected directly to the grid and they actually sell the excess power they generate to their power companies and then buy back what they need when their own systems aren't operating.

Three examples highlight the financial advantages of ecological design: The 1987 Internationale Nederlanden (ING) Bank headquarters in Amsterdam uses only 10 percent of the energy of its predecessor and has cut worker absenteeism by 15 percent because employees like coming to work and get sick less often. The combined savings equals $3.4 million per year. Homes in a California subdivision with solar heating and bike paths are now worth 12 percent more than homes in nearby conventional neighborhoods. And finally, an affordable housing development in Texas cut household utility bills by $450 a year by using efficient appliances and solar heating while adding only $13 a month to mortgage payments.

We'll talk about energy credits, a practical solution to promoting alternative energy sources, and other advantages of renewable energy in Chapter Six.

Sustainable Step #4:
Heal your home

I've mentioned sick building syndrome (also called "multiple chemical sensitivities" or MCS) several times in this book. A large portion of people who develop this condition do so right in their own homes.

MCS can be a serious problem, and there is no cure to the condition, so avoiding the pollutants is a necessity for MCS sufferers. Since MCS results from reaching a personal limit for processing environmental toxins, everyone is potentially at risk. The good news is that, with proper modifications, almost any home can be made healthy. Often, the fixes are fairly simple and inexpensive.

Multiple chemical sensitivities develop in some people when pollutants cause them to lose tolerance and react strongly to even minute levels of toxins in the environment. Reactions can include a variety of symptoms like the ones I've experienced: headaches, chronic cough, dizziness, sensitivity to odors, difficulty concentrating, burning eyes, achy joints, fatigue and worse. These symptoms are almost always initially attributed to something other than the building, since we often don't expect our building to be making us ill. Sometimes occupants of the building find relief almost immediately upon leaving the building and sometimes it takes much longer for them to recover. Frequently those symptoms worsen the more time they spend in the building.

If you're experiencing any of these symptoms that you can connect directly to your home, check to determine if any of the known causes of MCS may apply.

The Environmental Protection Agency says MCS can be caused by:

- Inadequate ventilation, especially when inadequate levels of outdoor air are circulated into the building;
- Indoor contaminants, including volatile organic compounds from adhesives, paints, carpeting, upholstery, manufactured wood products (not only in furniture, but in flooring and cabinetry), pesticides and cleaning products; outdoor contaminants, including pollutants from automobile exhaust, plumbing vents and building exhausts from bathrooms and kitchens that enter through air intake vents, windows and other openings; and
- Biological contaminants like molds, fungi, bacteria, pollen and viruses. These can breed in ducts, humidifiers and drain pains, or in damp carpets, wall materials, insulation, or ceiling tiles.

If you've recently done any remodeling, especially if you've installed any new carpeting or any type of flooring with particle board underlayment, or if you've installed new cabinetry made of particle board that contains high amounts of formaldehyde, or even installed new sheetrock with joint compounds, these could be the cause of your problems.

The EPA recommends removing the source of the contaminants, and this is what worked for me. This could include cleaning of heating and air conditioning systems, filters, and ductwork. It may be necessary to change moldy ceiling tiles and sheetrock. A drastic and expensive final measure may involve complete removal of the offending materials.

The seven things you can do now to heal your home and make it a "well building":

1. **Remove the carpet:** Carpet traps dust, mold, phthalate particles, pesticides and other toxins commonly used in lawns and gardens. Wood, tile or stone floors can be kept much cleaner, which is also healthier. If you want to "warm up" your floors, you can use organic cotton or wool rugs that can be taken outside and cleaned or washed.

2. **De-chlorinate the water:** As I mentioned in Chapter Three, chlorine from tap water is absorbed through your skin and lungs, especially during a hot shower. So it makes sense to filter your drinking and bathing water, but also consider a saline system for your pool if you have one. These systems use sodium chloride (table salt) to keep your pool clean at about one-sixth the chlorine content of a pool using regular chlorine. Saline systems also keep your hair from turning green while sharply reducing a major source of chlorine absorption through the skin. One helpful website for saline pool systems is www.salinepoolsystems.com.

3. **Insulate, insulate, insulate:** The tighter your house is, the less energy you'll consume to heat and cool it and the fewer outdoor pollutants can get inside. There are numerous types of nontoxic insulation, including cellulose and Icynene, that are safe and do not outgas.

continued on the next page

The seven things you can do now to heal your home and make it a "well building" continued

4. **Replace your mattress:** As I mentioned in Chapter Four, the formaldehyde and flame-retardant fumes that outgas from standard foam mattresses are just plain bad for you. These fumes can adversely affect your health, and you can't avoid them because your face and body are touching or only inches away for several hours a night. Buy an organic mattress even if you can't make any other investments to heal your house.

5. **Dump the artificials** (fragrances, cleaning supplies, personal care): All artificial personal care products, fragrances and cleaning supplies contain toxic ingredients, some of which can cause serious health problems for you and leave residual effects in your house. Conventional cleaning supplies can be exceptionally toxic. Read more about these in Chapters Three and Four.

6. **Bake out the bad stuff:** High heat in the house will speed outgassing of new construction materials and furniture, and will also stop the growth of mold spores. See Debra Lynn Dadd's technique in this chapter for accelerating offgassing and cleansing your home.

7. **Open the windows (ventilate):** Yes, I know we just said insulate, insulate, insulate. But it's equally important to regularly ventilate, since air quality in the average American home is far worse that outdoor air quality, precisely because our homes are so much more airtight in the twenty-first century. You can help outgas fumes from construction materials, carpets and furniture by simply opening the windows on mild days and letting fresh air circulate through your home for a few minutes a day. There are also new, quieter ventilation systems on the market that will ensure fresh air keeps circulating.

One of the easiest solutions is improved ventilation. Often this will be sufficient since building materials generally outgas in large amounts when they are new and in decreasing amounts as they age.

In her book, *Home Safe Home*, Debra Lynn Dadd recommends a relatively simple and cheap solution: A "bake-out" to remove volatile gases and cure the materials into an inert form.

The steps:

1. Remove all people, pets and plants.
2. Close all doors and windows.
3. Turn up central heat as far as it will go (or use space heaters).
4. At the end of each 24-hour period, open the doors and windows and air your home out completely. Use a fan if necessary.
5. Sniff around and check for odors. Determine if they are gone, or if you need another day of baking.

Dadd says the process can be completed in as little as one day and rarely takes more than four days.

No doubt you've heard of houses being abandoned or even torn down because of toxic contamination. Those stories are true, but the cases are rare. It's reassuring to know that most sick buildings are fixable and the "fixes," like baking your house and adding ventilation, aren't difficult or expensive in the vast majority of cases.

What You Need To Know

- Before you start any house project, carefully evaluate your needs. Upgrading an existing home is usually more environmentally sound than new construction, no matter how "green" the new house will be.
- Simple landscaping changes can make your home much more energy efficient.
- Paying attention to sun orientation, prevailing winds and the elements, and addressing them with landscaping, can keep your indoor climate more comfortable with less energy expenditure.
- If you are remodeling, building an addition or constructing a new home, look for a green contractor who is willing to use sustainable building practices and minimize or even eliminate the use of toxic construction materials.
- Keep close watch over construction activities to ensure your wishes are followed.
- Consider alternative energy sources for existing structures and new construction, if they are appropriate to your locale.
- If you have "sick building" symptoms, remove what you can, use natural sealers to stop the problem and consider "baking" your house to eliminate many problems.

PART III

A Sustainable Future

CHAPTER 6

Energy Sustainability: Time for Renewal

"America is addicted to oil."
—President George W. Bush

LIVING IN SOUTH FLORIDA and Park City, Utah, I have already seen the impact that a hotter planet is having on weather patterns—stronger hurricanes in the summers and lighter snowpack in the winters. To me, the climate change caused by the tons of carbon we are putting into the atmosphere each day is already deeply personal. This past winter, my young daughter asked me whether I thought there would still be snow to ski on when she was grown up. Skiing is a real passion for my family—we ski more than 20 days per year in a typical season, so the question really hit hard. That day, I decided to do what I could to reduce my net contribution to the problem, and set the goal at a zero net contribution to global warming.

First, I needed a real measurement of my personal environmental impact from energy use, and I found that carbon emissions were the best practical measure. My so-called "carbon footprint" measures the carbon dumped into the atmosphere and ocean from my existence. Since carbon is easy to measure, the major greenhouse gas, and a great indicator of other environmental impacts, I decided to offset my carbon footprint—and that of my family—as fully as possible, and to find the most convenient and cost-effective way to do so.

I found out that it is much easier than I ever thought to offset my total carbon emissions. I did many things around my home that I am going to tell you about, and I also tried to make up for the carbon-producing activities that I could not stop by purchasing carbon offsets—which operate like environmental "get out of jail free" passes.

My research revealed several very useful web-based services that can calculate the carbon emissions that you are causing by living in the modern world. The "big three" carbon-emitting activities we all engage in are home electrical power, car travel and air travel.

All of the services I found work on the basic principle of paying for credits which certify either a clean power source, such as wind, or an offset to the amount of carbon emitted, such as energy efficiency or reforestation (planting trees offsets carbon in the air because trees absorb carbon as they grow). Some of these websites, such as www.terrapass.com, focus exclusively on automobiles, with three sizes to choose from, while others such as www.renewablechoice.com and www.3phases.com are dedicated to providing clean power options to business and residential consumers.

The most comprehensive and cost-efficient of these carbon offset services is www.carbonfund.org. Using their handy "carbon calculator," I determined my current carbon footprint. This exercise, which took about one minute, determined my carbon use from the big three, home electricity, automobile use, and air travel. Then it offered several simple options for donating to offset this carbon footprint, along with the cost of each option. I choose to offset all of my family's carbon emissions, which costs about $99 per year for a typical person (mine was more because of two houses and lots of work-related air travel). Carbonfund.org is very cost-efficient because it operates as a low overhead non-profit, so it can buy carbon offset credits more cheaply and offer tax deductibility to consumers. For less than the cost of an airplane ticket, I had offset my family's entire carbon footprint in about five minutes.

But I didn't stop there. I conducted a quick review of ways that I could reduce my use of the "big three," saving even more pollution from entering the atmosphere. On principle, I cancelled one of the many airplane trips on my schedule (to pay for the carbon credits), and did the meeting by telephone conference instead. Based on the success of that meeting, I then cut about 20 percent of my remaining air travel for the year out completely.

I then went through my home and turned up the thermostat one or two degrees and unplugged the unused chargers, which I had learned continue to use power even when they're not charging. Those two steps took another five minutes and can save up to 8 percent of electrical power use for a typical home using electrical air conditioning.

Garden of Life, in its quest for greater environmental sustainability and good corporate citizenship, decided to move 100 percent of its energy purchases to renewable wind power, through 3Phases Energy. This company sells 100 percent renewable wind credits so you can buy energy from the wind without changing your power company or installing a windmill in your back yard!

You simply buy credits for the percentage of your energy use you want to offset and continue paying your current power bill. 3Phases certifies that electricity going into the grid from their wind farms is the power that you are buying, and that the money goes toward further investment in green power generating capacity. Some forward-thinking power providers, such as mine in Utah, Utah Power and Light, have programs where you can buy wind power directly as an option on your regular bill. In Park City, we get our power directly through Utah Power and Light from a wind farm just across the border near Evanston, Wyoming.

ENERGY – TIME FOR RENEWAL

The next logical step in our journey toward sustainability is keeping the fishbowl clean. Our fishbowl is Earth, the only known place in the universe where the delicate conditions are right to sustain life. We can help keep it that way by curbing our personal dependence on non-renewable energy sources.

It's time for renewal.

Our future is inextricably linked with renewable energy. To survive as a society and as a species, we simply need to move away from non-renewable sources of energy during our lifetimes. "Non-renewable" is a complex term for a simple concept: It means energy that we take out of the ground as liquids, gases and solids that can't be replaced. At the moment, crude oil (petroleum) is the only naturally occurring liquid fossil fuel.

Coal, petroleum, natural gas and propane require 300 to 400 million years of decomposition of the buried, heated and pressurized remains of plants and animals that lived millions of years ago to create fossil fuels. Our consumption of fossil fuels is unsustainable because we are consuming the reserves at a pace far, far faster than new stores can be formed.

Other major sources of energy come from uranium and plutonium, minerals mined and used in nuclear power plants. While these are not fossil fuels, uranium and plutonium stores are limited, so they are considered non-renewable energy sources. It's extremely difficult and dangerous to store uranium waste from nuclear power plants, which remains radioactive for more than 1,000 years, so their disposal presents an additional environmental problem.

The process of recovering fossil fuels from deep in the earth and then burning their carbon is unnatural and enormously harmful to earth, water and air.

Coal mining requires deep excavation and wide devastation above ground, not to mention the danger to the workers, to bring the coal to the surface, largely for use in power generating plants.

Exploring for gas and oil disrupts land, ocean and animal habitats. Oil spills, which are common in oil drilling operations, take years to clean up.

Refining petroleum products to create gasoline, diesel and heating oil creates additional air pollution and risks of land contamination from spills.

And transporting it to the consumer further adds to the pollution chain.

The damage doesn't end with the manufacturing process. When we burn gasoline in our cars or we turn on the lights and consume electrical power generated by coal-burning plants, we are contributing to the emission of greenhouse gases (primarily carbon dioxide and water vapor) that trap the heat of the sun in the earth's atmosphere.

Why is this a problem? Because global warming is not a theory, it's fact.

Globally, we're putting 7 billion metric tons of carbon dioxide into the air each year. That's more than fives times the amount of carbon dioxide emissions in 1950.

To get that down to personal terms, the average American household produces 24 tons of greenhouse gases each year. The U.S. emits almost twice as much fossil fuel-generated carbon dioxide as any other country in the world.

It's not encouraging when the U.S. Department of Energy issues a statement that says, "Fossil fuels—coal, oil and natural gas—currently provide more than 85 percent of all the energy consumed in the United States, nearly two-thirds of our electricity and virtually all of our transportation fuels. Moreover, it is likely that the nation's reliance on fossil fuels to power an expanding economy will actually increase over at least the next two decades even with aggressive development and deployment of new renewable and nuclear technologies."

The problems of global warming aren't a matter of a change of a fraction of a degree or a thousandth of an inch of sea level rising. Scientists tell us that the effects of greenhouse gases are exponential. That means every seemingly tiny changes can have large cumulative effects as the severity of storms increases, coral reefs die, water levels rise, snowpack decreases, and plant and animal ecosystems begin to fail.

As oceans absorb carbon dioxide from the atmosphere, the acidity of the oceans increases. An international team of 27 researchers reporting in the January 2006 issue of *Discover* forecast that at the current rate of carbon absorption, the ocean would become so acidic by the end of this century (from current pH 8.1 to 7.7) that many small marine creatures that comprise the basis of the food chain would simply dissolve.

If you want to learn more about global warming, visit the EPA's site www.epa.gov/globalwarming, the Sierra Club's comprehensive information site at www.sierraclub.org/globalwarming, www.realclimate.org for a more scientific dialog, or www.worldviewofglobalwarming.com to see pictures of the effects of global warming from around the world.

While the evidence on global warming is concerning, there is a future for us if we make some important changes now, starting with the way we consume energy.

Renewable energy is still in its infancy, and there are some very encouraging developments in this exciting field. Solar, wind, hydropower and alternative automobile fuels are hopeful steps in the right direction to reduce our dependence on fossil fuels. There are other even better technologies on the way.

In this chapter, I'll show you some simple ways that you can use renewable energy sources that take advantage of the technology that is now available and will, over time, contribute to the development of technologies that will make them the answer to our energy problems.

What You Can Do–
8 Sustainable Steps

Starting with natural electricity, here are the simple steps you can take to help reduce our dependence on fossil fuels and other non-renewable energy sources.

1. Buy natural electricity
2. Live near work
3. Slay the vampires
4. Change by degrees
5. Think globally, buy locally
6. Use power alternatives
7. Tune your car and save
8. Go hybrid

Sustainable Step #1:
Buy natural electricity

What's natural electricity? In short, it's power generated from a renewable source. One type of natural electricity is already well-established in the U.S., with water and gravity as its source.

Hydropower

Water power provides 97 percent of the renewable energy available in the United States, producing enough electricity to serve the needs of 28 million residential customers. This is equal to all the homes in Wisconsin, Michigan, Minnesota, Indiana, Iowa, Ohio, Missouri, Nebraska, Kansas, North and South Dakota, Kentucky, and Tennessee.

Hydropower is clean, leaves behind no residue and is efficient. It converts 90 percent of the available energy into electricity at about one-quarter of the cost of fossil fuel-powered electrical generation.

Use of hydropower prevents the burning of 22 billion gallons of oil or 120 million tons of coal each year—and that's an important savings in terms of greenhouse gases.

Wind

This one is my favorite. Wind power comprises only about 1 percent of the energy produced in the U.S., but its rapid growth (23 to 30 percent in each of the last five years) and its clean, cheap, abundant and ever-renewable nature make it a natural consideration for the power of the future.

The American Wind Energy Association says there is enough wind sweeping across the U.S. to supply all our power needs. North Dakota alone could provide 40 percent of our needs—and the wind farms can be installed on top of traditional grazing and agricultural lands, doubling the efficiency of agricultural land use. Realistically, though, experts estimate only about 6 percent of the U.S. energy needs will be provided by wind in the year 2020—about equal to the country's current hydropower capacity.

So why aren't we all basking in clean, cheap wind-generated electricity? The economic incentives are not quite compelling enough to attract large-scale investment in this exciting field. Windmills must be built and the delivery grid expanded to bring the wind power from the windiest sections of the country to the electricity-hungry urban areas. That's where purchasing renewable energy from carbon credits (also called green tags or wind certificates) can help the most—by creating the economic demand that will create new supply.

Wind power may still be the wave of the future, especially if more people are willing to fund this and other renewable energy sources by buying carbon credits, as I have.

Go carbon zero

The average American household is responsible for at least 10 tons of carbon dioxide emissions annually through energy use at home and for transportation. Add in purchases and the other activities of daily living, and the average carbon footprint is 24 tons a year.

Carbon credits are a cost-effective way to reduce your carbon footprint, or even wipe it out if you wish. By offsetting the excesses in your carbon footprint, you become a part of the solution to climate change.

These credits, or "green tags," go to fund the purchase of clean power or offset projects such as energy efficiency or reforestation. When a windmill puts electrons into the grid, the cost of generating that power (including the capital costs to build the windmill) is slightly higher than simply burning fossil fuels, at least at present. Green tags pay for the difference, and the electrons generated by wind don't know the difference.

As with organic foods, certification is critical to make sure that you are really getting clean power for your green tags. Buy them through a trustworthy organization such as Carbonfund.org, 3Phases, or Renewable Choice and look for the Green e-certification program.

Hero Profile: Carbonfund.org

Carbonfund.org is a nonprofit organization dedicated to offsetting carbon emissions through certified renewable power credits to purchase wind power instead of fossil fuel power, efficiency projects to reduce energy use, or through reforestation projects to plant new trees which stabilize carbon from the air as they grow. This organization is a hero to me because of its efficiency. It maintains low overhead and offsets a ton of carbon entering the atmosphere at 50 percent to 80 percent of the cost of other organizations. Donations are tax-deductible, so it's cost efficient as well. Learn how to offset your carbon footprint for around $99 per year at www.carbonfund.org.

Sustainable Step #2:
Live near work

This one doesn't take a lot of time to figure out. If you're commuting 30 or 40 miles a day to work, you are putting a lot of greenhouse gases into the air each day.

Commuting is expensive in terms of fuel and maintenance as well as in environmental terms. Long commutes also take an emotional toll and use time that could otherwise be spent on more fulfilling pursuits.

You may have to do some searching, but you might discover that a job closer to home, even if it pays less, may pay off in terms of personal health, environmental health and quality of life.

Or you may decide it is practical to move closer to your job. Even with the costs of moving, this could pay off economically and environmentally.

If a new job close to home or moving closer to work aren't in the cards, consider public transportation, which may not be 100 percent green, but is more fuel efficient than driving alone in your car. Carpooling is a greener alterative and many cities now have HOV or high-occupancy-vehicle lanes that encourage carpooling and give back the reward of faster commute times.

Sustainable Step #3:
Slay the vampires

No doubt your home is full of electric appliances like televisions, CD players, VCRs and DVD players, phone chargers and lots of other things that you plug into the wall and then forget about.

You may think they're "off," but they're not! Right now, your TV and other electronic appliances can each be drawing 2 to 10 watts of power while they are plugged in, even when they're turned off.

The California Energy Commission estimates that the average California household has between 10 and 20 external power supplies that cost the homeowner as much as $75 in wasted electricity each year. So, in a move intended to spark a nationwide movement, the commission has set new standards, effective this year, that will require appliances in the "off" position to use no more than three watts.

In terms of the bigger picture, experts estimate that residential consumers in the United States spend more than $5 billion annually on standby power—about 5 percent of all electricity consumed in the country.

To save yourself from these energy vampires, put your appliances on a power strip with one "off" switch that you can shut down when they're not in use. Energy Star™ appliances consume no more than half a watt of electricity when they are not turned on.

Beware of these other energy vampires:

1. Your computer consumes electricity equal to three 100-watt light bulbs when it is on. Turning it off when you're not using it saves as much as turning off the lights.

2. Refrigerator coils are another big energy drain that even the most energy-conscious citizens often overlook. Vacuuming your refrigerator coils at least twice a year improves energy efficiency.

3. Keeping your freezer full saves energy. Freezers work more efficiently when there are frozen goods in them to aid in keeping things cold.

4. Keeping your hot water heater set at no more than 120 degrees can save 10 percent of the operating cost for this energy-intensive appliance.

5. Just turning off your lights when you're not in the room can save on your lighting bill. It's a learned behavior, but a worthwhile one when you consider that the average household could save 5 to 10 percent of its energy bill by this one simple measure. According to the U.S. Department of Energy, one-third of our energy dollars go to lighting and appliances, not including heating water and using refrigeration.

BRIGHT VAMPIRES: OLD LIGHT BULBS

Replacing your conventional light bulbs with compact fluorescents will save you money and reduce your power needs.

Here's an excellent chart from www.healthgoods.com that gives you a comparison of the savings:

Compare

	Compact Fluorescent Lamp	Incandescent Bulb
Energy Used	20 Watts	75 Watts
Light Output	1200 Lumens	1180 Lumens
Lamp Life	10,000 Hours	750 Hours
Energy Use	200kWh	750kWh
Lamp Replacements	0	12
Original Lamp Cost	$18.00	$0.75
Lamp Replacement Cost	0	$9.00
Energy Cost @ 9¢/kWh	$18.00	$67.50
10,000 Hour Total Cost	$36.00	$77.25

You saved $41.25 over 10,000 hours of lamp operation on one bulb!
Potential savings at these other kWh electric rates per bulb
5¢/$19.25   7¢/$30.25   11¢/$52.25   13¢/$63.25   15¢/$74.25

The Environmental Impact
Reduction in acid rain, greenhouse and smog gases*
Carbon Dioxide–605 lbs.   Sulfur Dioxide–2.2 lbs.   Nitrous Oxide–0.4 lbs.
based on EPA kWh coefficients

The Department of Energy says that if every household in America installed just one compact fluorescent light bulb, we'd save enough energy to light 7 million homes and reduce greenhouse gas emissions equivalent to 1 million cars.

Full-spectrum compact fluorescent bulbs cost a bit more, but they can provide you with substantial health benefits from the full-spectrum light they provide, making them worth the extra initial cost.

Sustainable Step #4:
Change by degrees

Two degrees can make a tremendous difference. Turning down your thermostat in winter and turning it up in summer just two degrees can go a long way toward lowering your power consumption.

For every two degrees you raise your cooling system temperature (between 70 and 80 degrees) you save 6 to 8 percent in cooling consumption, and for every two degrees you lower your heating temperature (between 60 and 72 degrees) you save about 6 percent of your heating consumption. Those savings can add up.

You and your family probably won't notice a major difference between 72 and 74 degrees in summer or between 70 and 68 degrees in winter, but your pocketbook—and the environment—will.

The Department of Energy recommends keeping your indoor temperatures at 78 degrees in summer and 68 degrees in winter for a savings of up to 20 percent in your heating costs compared to where most thermostats are set today.

Better yet, buy a programmable thermostat and set it to fit your lifestyle— adjusting temperatures when you're asleep or not at home. This one-time investment of less than $100 can save you thousands of dollars in energy costs over the years.

Best of all, in milder climates, use fans instead of air conditioning and more energy-efficient heating systems like heat pumps and save a bundle.

Simple Step #5:
Think globally, buy locally

Here's an eye-popping statistic I ran across in my research: Transporting one pound of asparagus from Chile to New York uses 73 pounds of fuel energy and releases 4.7 pounds of carbon dioxide into the atmosphere.

Buying locally grown foods saves energy by eliminating the need for costly food transportation.

Local farmers' markets and food co-ops frequently have high-quality locally grown products that are also healthier because they haven't lost nutrients in a lengthy shipping process. As a bonus, many of these products are organic or at least grown with minimal pesticide use.

You can also increase the market for locally grown goods by asking your natural foods supermarket or even your ordinary supermarket to buy locally grown goods.

Sustainable Step #6:
Use power alternatives

The sunlight that fell on the roads in the U.S. last year contained roughly as much energy as all the fossil fuels consumed last year in the entire world. Best of all, sunlight is totally sustainable, non-polluting and free!

You've no doubt picked up a package of solar garden lights at your local discount or home supply store. This is just one of the simplest examples of how easy—and inexpensive—it can be to incorporate alternative technologies into your lifestyle.

To me, these little lights symbolize a shift in the consciousness of our society and a place where technology has met consumer demand in an elegant and practical way. For $30 or less, you or I can light up an area and never, ever have to pay a power bill for it or worry about it again, other than to replace a rechargeable battery every couple of years.

Everywhere I turn, there are new alternatives based on increasingly reliable and inexpensive technologies that take us a step further away from fossil fuel dependence every day. Real Goods remains the best source I have found for solar products and information. Visit them at www.realgoods.com to see the latest in solar solutions. To find a contractor who can install solar products, visit www.findsolar.com.

Here are a few options:

Solar hot water: Whole-house solar power remains a technological challenge at present, but solar hot water is within the reach of most households in the U.S. and can help you save 25 to 33 percent of your power bill. There are several different types of systems that can be retrofitted to existing homes, and most of them are unobtrusive enough to pass muster even in restricted communities. Solar water heaters are reasonably priced

($1,000 to $3,500), can show paybacks in four to seven years depending upon the fuel displaced (electric or gas), and can replace two-thirds or more of the conventional fossil fuel energy systems used in conventional water heating.

Solar attic fan: These fans are reasonably priced (in the $300 to $400 range) and can ventilate attic spaces and exchange cool night air for hot daytime air, reducing your cooling costs, at no cost at all for power.

Solar-powered flashlights, radios and chargers: These gained popularity a few years ago as potential survival tools and I can tell you they come in very handy when the power goes out, as it has recently at my home due to Florida hurricanes. You can find these items for $30 or less, sometimes even in combination. They work well and are reliable when you need them most. You may find some that have handles to crank when there is insufficient sun.

Solar battery and cell phone chargers: These almost eliminate the need for "always on" chargers.

Solar garden accessories: Ranging from pond and swimming pool filters to a wide array of outdoor lighting and even fans, pool heaters and more, these have almost become standard fare. Why pay for power when you can get it free from the sun?

Rooftop wind turbines to power small appliances: If you've got an average wind speed of 10 mph, one of these small (46-inch diameter) turbines can give you about 20 kilowatt-hours of power monthly. That's enough to power lighting and the occasional small appliance. The new models are quiet, so they're acceptable for urban and suburban settings, and they are reasonably priced at about $750. Watch for wind power to become more available and to spread to more household uses. The downside of these home windmills is that they require battery storage, which is not the best choice for the environment at this time. An excellent overview of the current state of the art in rooftop wind power generation is available at www.wikipedia.com (just type in Wind Power as a search).

Solar Homes for Everyone

Whole-house solar technology is now a practical reality.

The U.S. Department of Energy's Building America program has designed and constructed 26,000 "net-zero-energy" homes in dozens of high-energy demand cities along the East and West coasts. They are super energy efficient, producing much of their electricity for free using solar panels on the roof.

While the new construction costs 10 to 20 percent more than conventional construction, DOE estimates that net-zero-energy homes will cost no more than comparable conventional homes in the next decade. When you add in the tiny monthly energy bills, net-zero-energy homes are a good investment even today.

Among the net-zero test homes is a development of 90 solar homes in Clear Lake, California. At $250,000 to $330,000 each, the 1,400- to 1,900-square-foot homes are very competitive in that market.

Sustainable Step #7:
Tune your car and save

If your car is in perfect running order, it will run more efficiently and your gas consumption will drop.

Here are a few simple ways to boost gas mileage:

1. Check your tires weekly. Properly inflated tires can save 2 percent on gas consumption.

2. Get a tune-up and boost your miles per gallon by anywhere between 4 and 40 percent if your car has a serious problem, like a faulty oxygen sensor. Just replacing your air filter can increase your gas mileage by as much as 10 percent.

3. Take the roof rack off your car when you're not using it and stop gas-guzzling wind drag.

Four low-cost solar homes recently completed by Habitat for Humanity volunteers in Lenoir City, Tennessee, are fast-tracking renewable energy for low-income families. These small (1,000- to 1,200-square-foot) homes were built for approximately $100,000 each. This includes the cost of the solar systems and factors in the labor of the Habitat volunteers as though they were paid. These pleasant colonial homes with porches and shutters look like any suburban community, but their total energy bills average less than $25 a month.

The American Solar Energy Society maintains an excellent informational website at www.ases.org and also publishes a bimonthly magazine called *Solar Today* that covers all renewable energy technologies. To estimate your cost to go solar for part of your home electrical needs, visit www.findsolar.com, which also has a referral service that makes it easy to find a solar contractor in your area.

Sustainable Step #8:
Go hybrid

Please don't send your car to the junkyard and run out and buy a hybrid tomorrow, but when you *need* a new car, give hybrids, alternative fuels, flexible fuel tanks and other green options some serious consideration.

HYBRID VEHICLES

Gas-electric hybrids are an important part of the movement toward green transportation. I'll be the first to say they aren't *the* answer, but they're probably the best answer we have right now.

More and more models are becoming available every year, with Toyota and Honda leading the pack with the Prius, which gets 50 to 60 miles per gallon—about the same as my Vespa scooter—and the Insight, which gets similar gas mileage.

There are also several larger vehicles, like Ford's Escape, Mercury's Mariner, Mazda's Tribute, Lexus' RX 400h and Toyota's Highlander, which feature a hybrid drive system.

In addition, Honda Civics and Toyota Camrys are now available in hybrid models, and Toyota has promised that all of its models will eventually be available as hybrids.

At present, hybrid models cost between $3,500 and $6,000 more than comparable conventional vehicles. However, most of these vehicles qualify for tax credits and get to use the carpool lanes. With the high cost of gasoline, hybrids make sense for environmental and economic reasons.

Before you buy an automobile, consider your size needs very carefully. A hybrid SUV may get better mileage than its non-hybrid brother, but at about 25 miles per gallon these are less fuel efficient than smaller cars without a hybrid engine.

The government's fuel economy website, www.fueleconomy.gov, offers a wealth of information and allows you to compare mileage and other features of hybrids to help you make the best choice for you, your family and the environment.

A NOTE ON CAR INTERIORS

The inside of your car may be the single most polluted place you visit each day. Indoor air in automobiles is contaminated with two toxic chemicals known to cause liver damage, thyroid disruption, impaired learning, and early puberty (at least in laboratory animals—this would be unethical to test in humans). The primary culprits are the phthalates used to make plastic parts softer and PBDEs, which are used as flame retardants.

According to an excellent report by the nonprofit Ecology Center, the much higher levels of toxins inside your car or truck mean that 90 minutes of driving (a typical commute both ways for many people) is equivalent to exposure from a full eight hours at work.

Because these chemicals are volatile in heat, parking in the sun makes the problem dramatically worse. Laws are under consideration in many first-world countries to ban these chemicals altogether, and a few forward-thinking automakers, notably Volvo and BMW, have initiatives underway to phase out their use completely. Because I cannot tolerate the chemicals used in the production of hybrid car interiors, I drive a small Volvo when my Vespa is impractical. My car gets better mileage than a large hybrid vehicle, more than double the mileage of the small SUV it replaced, and has an interior made specifically to be free from harmful chemicals. View the full report on car interiors, including a list of the best and worst automakers based on windshield samples, at http://www.ecocenter.org/toxicatanyspeed.shtml.

Hero Profile: Toyota

Toyota is the second-largest automobile manufacturer in the world, and as a result their products contribute substantially to global warming and greenhouse gas emissions. The difference is that Toyota is doing something about it. Toyota has taken the lead in development of highly fuel-efficient, gas-electric hybrid motors, best represented by the popular Prius. I applaud this company's leadership in fuel efficiency. Now if they can just do something about phthalates, flame retardants and other chemicals sprayed on the inside. More on the Prius at www.toyotausa.com.

FLEXIBLE FUEL TANKS AND ALTERNATIVE FUELS

Flexible fuel tanks: These unique fuel tanks can run on a mix of 85 percent ethanol and 15 percent gasoline (E85), gasoline only, or any combination of the two. Flex fuel tanks are widely available in Ford, GM and Chrysler cars, vans and trucks. About 2.3 million flex fuel cars, vans, pickups and SUVs are on the road in the U.S., but only a small percentage of them actually use E85 because it is still difficult to find this fuel.

One hitch in the popularity of flex fuel vehicles is the shortage of a delivery system for E85. Ethanol stations are few and far between, so many flex fuel vehicle owners are forced to use straight gasoline at least part of the time. Most of the 619 stations are in the cornbelt in the Midwest, with Minnesota leading the list with 203 stations, so it's almost a "buy local" option there.

Hybrid vehicles are not available with flex fuel tanks, although some have been retrofitted with them.

Ethanol and E85: E85 is most often made from domestically produced corn-derived ethanol and costs 10 to 20 cents per gallon less than regular gasoline. An estimated 13 million gallons of E85 fuel were consumed in the United States in 2004. Besides corn, other renewable plant materials like wheat stalks, grasses and forestry waste can be used to make E85.

Many vehicles use small percentages of ethanol (typically 10 percent) to improve performance and reduce emissions.

Cars that use E85 get lower mileage per gallon—about 20 percent lower—but ethanol is currently about 20 percent cheaper than regular gasoline, so that's pretty much a washout. The advertised benefit of E85 is that it reduces greenhouse gas emissions by about 20 percent net.

The push for fuel from crops represented by E85 is deeply concerning to me. As an advocate for sustainable agriculture, I see the massive amounts of pesticides, herbicides, and (yes) petroleum-based fertilizers used to grow crops for fuel instead of food as an ecological disaster. Taken together, the production of biofuel from crops consumes more energy than it produces, missing my definition of sustainable. Conversion of farmland for fuel production will reduce arable land for food production and increase dependence on imported food, which just seems like a very bad idea.

Biodiesel: This domestically produced, renewable fuel can be manufactured from vegetable oils, animal fats, or recycled restaurant greases. Biodiesel is safe, biodegradable, and reduces serious air pollutants, such as particulates, carbon monoxide, hydrocarbons and air toxins. Blends of 20 percent biodiesel with 80 percent petroleum diesel (B20) can generally be used in unmodified diesel engines. Biodiesel can also be used in its pure form (B100), but it may require certain engine modifications to avoid maintenance and performance problems and may not be suitable for wintertime use.

There are only 348 biodiesel stations the U.S., but that's a little misleading since many users have arranged for private delivery at home or at a place of business. Stay informed as this renewable fuel gains traction at the National Biodiesel Board's website: www.biodiesel.org.

Other alternative fuels: In addition to ethanol and biodiesel, there are cars in development and a handful on the road that run on hydrogen, natural gas, propane, methanol and electricity. You can learn more about all types of alternative fuels at www.eere.energy.gov.

Neighborhood vehicles: Glorified golf carts that will go up to 35 mph and travel 40 to 60 miles on an electric charge, electric motorcycles, scooters and bicycles are great ways to be more mobile, do your local errands and reduce your carbon footprint. More information on these is available at www.nesea.org/greencarclub.

What You Need To Know

- There are many simple ways to conserve energy and reduce and offset your personal contributions to greenhouse gases.
- Reducing your dependence on fossil fuel-based energy and switching to renewable energy sources can make important contributions to energy efficiency.
- Setting your thermostat two degrees differently can save up to 8 percent on your power bill.
- There are dozens of inexpensive alternative power products on the market today.
- Keeping your car in perfect working order can dramatically improve gas consumption and emissions.
- Driving less aggressively can decrease fuel consumption dramatically.
- You can offset your excess energy consumption or even all of your energy consumption and greenhouse gas emissions by buying carbon credits.
- Hybrid vehicles are steps in the right direction toward sustainable transportation choices.

CHAPTER 7

The Big Picture

*"We can not solve problems at the same
level of awareness that created them."*
—Albert Einstein

IT'S BEEN MORE THAN A DECADE since my first bite at the organic apple, and my journey has taken me from selfishly health-conscious to impassioned green advocate, step by sustainable step. I've changed my diet, my clothes, my home, my furniture, my car, my shampoo, and many of my consumption habits. I've even changed my professional focus and volunteer activities. Although still far from perfect, my path has become permanently greener, and a driving force for my choice of this path came from my own young daughters.

Parenthood changes our perspective. Children force us to think beyond ourselves and help us gain an appreciation for the future. We want the best for them and want them to have an even better life than we have had.

My kids are growing up pretty green. They have eaten a diet that is as organic as practical for their entire lives. They live in a green home built without offgassing materials. They don't often drink sodas or eat candy— it's simply not in the house. They usually read instead of watching television and get to spend lots of time outdoors in nature.

And yet they are concerned.

Will we have a chance to teach our own children to ski?

Will our Florida house be underwater by the time we are adults?

Will we still be able to catch fish when we're grown up?

These are just a few of the questions I've had from my own daughters over the past year. Yes, part of the reason is my research for this book has been part of our dinner table conversations. But these really are the right questions for us to ask, and here's my favorite:

What can we do to make sure that nature is still there when we grow up?

That is the question that inspired me to write this book.

Experts disagree on some specifics, but are unanimous in their urgings that we need to start now with positive steps to reduce global warming. Highly populated developing nations are not going to slow down their economic growth, making the consumption problem potentially worse. Al Gore's research has led him to believe that we have 10 years before the problem of global warming is irreversible. That's not much time.

But it's not too late. Powerful trends are converging on the problems of the unsustainable path that we are on. Taken together, they have the potential to create a brighter future by taking on the single biggest issue of our times head on.

THE RISE OF GREEN

Sustainability is an idea whose time has come. We know that we are at the limits of our resources, and we want to do things differently. Even without knowing what it might really mean, people want to live greener, especially if it can be done easily. Sustainability has been heartily embraced by cultural leaders, who are making it cool to be green. Green is even patriotic, as we realize that our national security and the economic fate of our nation are linked to energy independence.

We are at the start of a green revolution. Sustainability issues are reaching a critical tipping point in our society, and hopefully just in time.

The resolve that we need to take action starts with awareness. And that awareness is dawning on us by the millions.

DOLLARS ARE GETTING GREENER

Each of us participates in the economy, choosing what to buy and where to buy it every single day of our lives. In our consumer-driven economy, those daily economic choices have huge downstream implications. And those implications are becoming an important part of the purchase decision-making process for millions of consumers who are now factoring their values into the purchase equation. Paying a small premium for organic fiber creates the economic incentive for a farmer to switch his land to organic production. Buying fair-trade coffee means that the grower will get a fair wage for her labor.

The new consumer consciousness for sustainability is changing the economic landscape.

Products that once were unavailable or considered exotic are now right in the center of the mainstream. Organic produce, once the realm of small health food stores, is now available in almost any supermarket. Alternative health services, once seen as unconventional, are now a component of virtually any sizeable medical center or university medical school. Recycling, once a major effort involving trips to distant recycling centers and prodigious cleaning and sorting, is now available curbside in virtually every U.S. town and city. And yoga classes, once considered weird, are now taught in almost every YMCA, health club and college in the nation.

This boom in demand for healthy-living products and services is at the vanguard of a green revolution in how consumers are voting their dollars. These companies and their products are there only because of consumer demand. And that demand is growing.

Business leaders like Marci Zaroff of Under the Canopy or Beaver Theodosakis of Prana have created an entire new industry, based on their own creativity and on consumer demand for fashionable, comfortable clothing made from natural and organic fibers.

Even old-school giants like the automobile industry are being touched by greener dollars, as evidenced by the boom in sales of gas-electric hybrid cars that get up to 60 miles per gallon. People around the country are waiting in line to pay a premium for these more fuel-efficient vehicles.

THE BIG GREEN RIPPLE

People by the millions now understand that how they live and what they buy have a tremendous ripple effect on the world around them. Our purchases change the course of human activity by creating economic incentives that reward the providers of the products that we choose to buy. This insight into the ripple effect of purchases is reaching a tipping point in many industrialized countries around the world. And that ripple is turning distinctively green.

Oceans, fields and jungles are the beneficiaries of this new consumer equation. Consider the Amazon. This incredible habitat is thought to be home to over half of the world's species. Unfortunately it is still being destroyed at a rapid rate. This is especially troubling because most of the nutrient value in the ecosystem is in the vegetation, which is burned or logged off leaving soil that is productive only for a few seasons before the destructive cycle starts again. Buying rainforest-friendly Amazon products like nuts and chocolate helps both preserve the forest ecosystem and create an economic incentive for the people living there to retain their jungle canopy.

The stock of large wild fish in our oceans has been depleted by over 90 percent in the past 50 years, lowering the levels of some species so much that they can never recover. This is called "collapse" of a population, and it means that more species will go the way of the great cod populations once off the coast of New England (so thick that boats had trouble pushing through them!) and the thriving sardine schools once off the coast of California. We used to view the ocean as an endless resource, but we are now realizing its limits. Again, your purchases can make a difference. Buying seafood from sustainable fisheries where catch is closely monitored to ensure breeding populations remain is an important way to make a difference. Sustainable fishing methods include trolling rather than netting, and size and catch restrictions to guard against overfishing. The Monterey Bay Aquarium runs an excellent website on marine sustainability issues at www.mbayaq.org.

Fair-trade coffee is one final example of the big green ripple. A typical coffee grower gets less than 2 percent of the final purchase price of a cup of coffee, and as a result has scant economic incentive to preserve the environment in which the coffee is grown. An organic, shade-grown, fair-trade certified coffee costs more but at least guarantees fair wages for the grower, a respect for the environment and a healthier, more sustainable product for you to consume. All you have to do is choose to pay the premium.

GREEN IS GOOD FOR BUSINESS

In 1776, Scottish economist Adam Smith published *The Wealth of Nations*, the seminal book on capitalism. It identified land (natural resources), labor (people), and capital (money) as the three key ingredients for a successful economy. The fourth necessary element was what Smith called the entrepreneur, the risk-taker who combines these elements into a successful economic enterprise. At a time when natural resources seemed absolutely unlimited, this model was nearly perfect, and it has been the basic model for the most successful economies in the world since it was published over 200 years ago.

At that time, the world had a population of less than 1 billion people, and fossil fuels had not yet been discovered.

Smith could not have foreseen a world where natural resources were in short supply and pollution from enterprise was risking the planet's very ability to sustain life.

But some of Smith's entrepreneurs are now factoring the environment into the equation. Sustainability as a business principle is on the rise. Smart companies are making their businesses greener. In many important segments of our economies, the entire business model is shifting to take into consideration the broader impacts business can have on the environment and on society. In Europe, it is standard practice to issue a sustainability report along with the traditional financial-driven annual report.

And it's not just healthy-living companies that are committed to making a difference. Sustainable practices are getting at least some attention at corporate giants like Ford, Ikea, Nike and even BP (which apparently has changed the meaning of BP from British Petroleum to Beyond Petroleum). Small companies like Garden of Life and hundreds of others are building sustainability into everyday business life: recycling paper, recycling batteries and cell phones, producing products with fewer petrochemical-based products, printing with vegetable inks and recyclable materials, using sustainable packaging materials, buying locally and supporting renewable energy by buying renewable energy credits.

Some business have chosen to take their commitment to sustainability even further by engaging in fair trade and business sustainability in the supply chain, leaving a smaller chemical footprint throughout the entire manufacturing process.

One non-governmental organization, Global Reporting Initiative (www.globalreporting.org), sets environmentally and socially responsible guidelines that more than 680 multinational corporations have voluntarily adopted.

The Equator Principles of 2003 provide a similar set of guidelines for financing development projects adopted by 23 member banks representing 80 percent of development financing, including banking giants CitiGroup, Bank of America and NSBC Holding.

Already the second wave of business sustainability is showing its face. It's the concept of moving from basic sustainability to "ecological, economic and social responsibility," says Andres Edwards in *The Sustainability Revolution*.

"The ecological, economic and equity components of sustainability are no longer viewed as competing but rather as complementary. The choice is not economic growth at the expense of the environment, but environmental protection, a vibrant economy and equitable resource distributions," Edwards wrote.

I'm sure Adam Smith, whose other eighteenth-century bestseller was *The Theory of Moral Sentiments*, would be proud to see his entrepreneurs adjusting to the new reality and incorporating sustainability into their capitalism.

GREEN POLITICS

Politics are turning green. While most parliamentary governments in Europe have had "Green" parties for decades, this is a new and explosive phenomenon on the American political scene. For a growing number of voters on both sides of the political spectrum, sustainability has become a critical issue. For some of us, it really is the ONLY issue—and certainly the only one posing a real threat to our lives and civilization.

I remember the terrifying experience of "duck and cover" drills in elementary school done in preparation for a potential nuclear attack. But global warming, rising ocean levels and ecological disaster are now far more terrifying because they have the real potential to end our society. A generation that grew up under the threat of nuclear war is realizing this potential all at once, and is shifting focus to a much larger and more urgent problem.

Green has become a patriotic color. Politicians from both parties are competing on sustainability proposals, especially in populous, powerful and trendsetting states such as California. For a new generation of politicians, being green is no longer a matter of political party. Being green has become a matter of political survival. Voters are increasingly rejecting the tired false tradeoffs of "jobs versus the environment" and insisting on sustainable solutions that take both into account from their elected officials. It is obvious to voters that our dependence on imported oil to fuel our economy makes us vulnerable. Our national security is at stake, and voters and the political leaders they elect are expressing their patriotism by working towards a sustainable society.

As environmental and natural resource issues take center stage in global politics, the opportunity for greater cooperation among nations will be driven by mutual self-interest. Collaboration will be essential to addressing sustainability on a global scale. As a result, sustainability issues will be a major driver of international politics for decades to come.

GREEN TECHNOLOGIES

Exciting developments in green technologies are on the horizon. Like global warming itself, these are happening faster than we could have ever predicted even a few years ago. California's "Hydrogen Highway" initiative, led by Governor Arnold Schwarzenegger (who has apparently retired the Hummer), has the potential to install a useable hydrogen infrastructure to the sixth-largest economy in the world that is the state of California over just the next few years. That means that once clean-burning hydrogen vehicles become commercially viable, you could get a fill-up.

The first hydrogen-powered motorcycle is on its way. The ENV bike (www.envbike.com), now under development, can go 50 miles per hour and travel 100 miles on a single tank of…air! This zero-emissions vehicle (unless you count a little pure water as an emission) will take the world by storm in 2007. Hydrogen-fueled cars will follow. Creating hydrogen from electrical power represents a remaining problem since most electricity generation is still based on burning fossil fuels. Generating truly pollution-free transportation fuels will require the expansion of our capacity to generate clean electricity from renewable resources.

With oil prices at record highs, the economic incentives for creating clean energy technology and capacity have never been stronger. Enough sunshine fell on our roads last year to meet all of our electrical power needs, with the right technology. Enough wind blows over Wyoming each year to power all of the western U.S. for a year, with the right infrastructure for capturing it. Solar, wind and other clean technologies just need to catch up.

Japan is leading the way in solar technology. This makes sense, since that island nation has no oil of its own and is totally dependent on imported oil to meet its current needs. The Japanese have already identified energy independence as a strategic priority, and are working on some exciting solutions, including holographic solar cells that are many times more efficient at converting the sun's rays to electrical power.

The ocean has unlimited power in the form of waves and tides, but harnessing it is the challenge. New prototype power plants float on or just below the surface and generate electrical power from the action of ocean waves turning a turbine. For now, the cost of production is a bit more than fossil fuels, but with the inevitable rise of oil costs, this should be at parity within the next decade or so.

Basic and applied research on renewable power and cleaner technologies is underway in most industrial countries around the world. Once

Stepping Toward Sustainability: Garden of Life

I've been involved with Garden of Life, a leading organic food and whole food supplement company, for several years, and I now serve as its CEO. This is a young company that has come a long way in the six short years it has been in existence.

Because Garden of Life is young and full of creative, energetic people, we were eager to bring a greater commitment to sustainability to the workplace. We recognize that no matter how careful we are to build sustainability into our products, good health cannot be achieved in isolation from the environment.

So we made some changes to our business practices.

Garden of Life offers health-positive natural foods that can create sustainable economies in areas of the world that would otherwise have to rely on extraction of natural resources to provide a livelihood for its people. The organic cacao in our new Rainforest Cacao Chocolate is harvested and processed in the jungles of Amazonian Ecuador by peoples who can earn a certified fair-trade

developed, new and economically viable clean technologies will be adopted worldwide at a rapid pace.

YOU AND ME

Have you ever wanted to change the world? Well, now's your chance. You can change it for the better with the foods you eat, the car you drive, and the way you pay your power bill. You can change the world by turning off the lights, passing on the Styrofoam cup and separating your trash. None of these steps toward a more sustainable lifestyle will break your budget, and the collective impact of these choices is enormous.

price for their labors, and thus value the diverse bounty of the jungle for its productivity rather than clear-cutting it for short-term crop production.

Our business operation requires us to use electrical power, which is normally achieved from the burning of fossil fuels. Fossil fuels such as coal, oil and natural gas give the environment a double-whammy, simultaneously burning an irreplaceable energy source and polluting the atmosphere and ocean. That's why Garden of Life buys 100 percent of our electricity needs from wind power, a pollution-free renewable resource. We are among the first companies of our size to make this full commitment to renewable power. While this adds expense to our business, it is worthwhile to save over 1 million pounds of carbon dioxide in the atmosphere and prevent the burning of 300 tons of coal per year as certified by the independent Green-E organization. There is more on Garden of Life's green initiatives available at www.gardenoflife.com.

These are small steps in light of our global sustainability challenge and we are far from perfect, but we feel that it is important to start somewhere and take these first steps.

CHANGE IS IN THE AIR

Now more than ever, it is clear that the world is small, and getting smaller. Each of the almost 6 billion inhabitants of this planet is connected by the very air that we breathe. If we want our children and future generations to keep breathing, we have to change.

And change is in the air.

A friend told me the story of walking along a beach near her home, where thousands of starfish had been stranded by a storm surge followed by an unusually low tide. A young boy was ferrying the doomed starfish back to safety at the water's edge. As the boy ran back and forth, a middle-aged tourist watched him. Eventually the man couldn't contain himself any longer.

She watched as he approached the boy, took him by the arm and asked, "What do you think you're doing? You can't possibly save them all."

The boy gazed directly into the cynical older man's eyes and replied with all the innocence of childhood. "I can make a difference. To this one," he said as he flipped a starfish back to the safety of the sea. "And this one, and this one…."

Change is in the air because we are making mindful choices that make a difference, one small step at a time. And that larger difference is already starting to change the world.

IN CLOSING…

So, where do you take it from here?

How can I make a difference?

What can we do to *make sure* nature is still there when our children grow up?

It is my sincere hope that this book has given you some answers to those questions and given you practical ways to act on your own good intentions. It was written to help empower you to live a better life—better for you and better for those who follow you. In my view, the stakes are so high that nothing on our political, economic or even personal agenda is more important than ensuring a sustainable future. Because sustainability is such a dynamic topic, you have my commitment to keep a resource site current with all latest developments at www.wellbuilding.com. Stay tuned there for the latest news and exciting future developments.

Welcome to a new way of life.

Resource and Product Guide

GENERAL RESOURCES

Garden of Life is a high-quality brand of whole food based supplements and organic foods available at health food stores, vitamin chains and natural supermarkets nationwide.

Dr. Joseph Mercola has a wealth of health, food and supplement information on his website: www.mercola.com.

Daliya Robson's website for nontoxic household furnishings: www.nontoxic.com.

Tom Foerstel's websites for organic products: www.organic.org; www.organiclinks.com.

Marci Zaroff's site for ecofashion: www.underthecanopy.com.

For sustainably harvested household products: www.seventhgeneration.com.

Natural Home and Garden magazine subscription information and some articles are available at the website: www.naturalhomeandgarden.com.

For information on renewable energy technologies and alternative fuel vehicles, visit the U.S. Department of Energy's division of energy efficiency and renewable energy: www.eere.gov.

CHAPTER 2: Sustainability from the Inside
NATURAL AND ORGANIC FOODS
Breads and baked goods (organic)

Food for Life Baking Co.: www.food-for-life.com
French Meadow Bakery: www.frenchmeadow.com
Nature's Path Foods: www.naturespath.com
Vita-Spelt: www.purityfoods.com

Food bars (whole grain, organic, sugar-free)

CocoChia Snack Fuel Bars: www.livingfuel.com
Living Food Bars by Garden of Life: www.gardenoflife.com

Kefir (a healthy fermented soybean product)

Amaltheia Dairy: www.amaltheiadairy.com
Helios Nutrition: www.heliosnutrition.com
Real Foods Market: www.realfoodsmarket.com

Coconut milk

Native Forest Organic Coconut Milk: www.edwardandsons.com
Thai Kitchen Coconut Milk: www.thaikitchen.com

Dairy products from cow's milk
(organic, no growth hormones or antibiotics)

Brown Cow Farm: www.browncowfarm.com
Joseph Mercola, D.O.: www.mercola.com
Natural by Nature: www.natural-by-nature.com
Organic Pastures Dairy Co.: www.organicpastures.com
Organic Valley: www.organicvalley.com
Peaceful Pastures: www.peacefulpastures.com
Real Foods Market: www.realfoodsmarket.com
Stonyfield Farm: www.stonyfield.com

Eggs (high omega-3 fatty acid content, free range and organic)
Eggland's Best: www.eggland.com
Gold Circle Farms: www.goldcirclefarms.com
Organic Valley: www.organicvalley.com

Red meats (organic and grass fed, hormone and antibiotic-free)
Baldwin Family Farms: www.baldwinfamilyfarms.com
Brady Ranch Exotic Meats: www.bradyranchmeats.com
Buffalo Guys: www.thebuffaloguys.com
Coleman Purely Natural Products: www.colemannatural.com
Homestead Healthy Foods: www.homesteadhealthyfoods.com
Maverick Ranch Natural Meats: www.maverickranch.com
Northstar Bison: www.northstarbison.com
Peaceful Pastures: www.peacefulpastures.com
Real Foods Market: www.realfoodsmarket.com
White Oak Pastures: www.whiteoakpastures.com
Wyoming Natural Products Co.: www.wyomingnatural.com

Poultry (free range, hormone and antibiotic free)
Bell & Evans: www.bellandevans.com
Oaklyn Plantation: www.freerangechicken.com
Peaceful Pastures: www.peacefulpastures.com
Rosie's Organic Chicken: www.petalumapoultry.com
Shelton's Poultry: www.sheltons.com

Fish (wild caught frozen or canned)
Ecofish: www.ecofish.com
Joseph Mercola, D.O.: www.mercola.com
Monterey Bay Aquarium: www.mbayaq.org/cr/seafoodwatch.asp
Real Foods Market: www.realfoodsmarket.com
Vital Choice Seafood: www.vitalchoice.com
Wild Planet: www.1wildplanet.com

Deli meat (organic, nitrate and nitrite-free)

Applegate Farms: www.applegatefarms.com

Vegetables (fresh, organic)

Earthbound Farm: www.ebfarm.com

Frozen fruits and vegetables

Cascadian Farms: www.cfarm.com

Organic tomato sauces and salsas

Muir Glen: www.muirglen.com

Seeds of Change: www.seedsofchange.com

Solana Gold Organics: www.solanagold.com

Coffee (organic, sustainably grown, fair trade)

Green Mountain Coffee Roasters: www.greenmountaincoffee.com

Organic Coffee Co.: www.organiccoffeecompany.com

Pura Vida Coffee: www.puravidacoffee.com

Oils

Bariani Olive Oil: www.barianioliveoil.com

Barlean's Organic Oils: www.barleans.com

Garden of Life: www.gardenoflife.com

Manitoba Harvest: www.manitobaharvest.com

Nutiva: www.nutiva.com

Omega Nutrition: www.omeganutrition.com

Rejuvenative Foods: www.rawoils.com

Spectrum Organic Products: www.spectrumorganics.com

Wilderness Family Naturals: www.wildernessfamilynaturals.com

Air and Water Filters

AllergyBuyers Club: www.allergybuyersclub.com

BPA Air Quality Solutions: www.breathepureair.com

Ecobaby Organics: www.ecobaby.com

Lifekind Products: www.lifekind.com

Nirvana Safe Haven: www.nontoxic.com

Priorities: www.priorities.com

Tomorrow's World: www.tomorrowsworld.com

Water Bottles

Corn Plastic Bottles: www.healthyhome.com

These bottles are made of NatureWorks corn-based plastic, and do not contain phthlates that can leach into your water. Some even come with built-in filters so you can drink filtered water on the go.

HDPE Water Bottles

Nalgene Outdoor: www.nalgene-outdoor.com

Make sure you use only HDPE versions of Nalgene bottles, since the more popular Lexan versions can leach BPA into your water.

Stainless Steel Water Bottles

Kleen Kanteen: www.greenfeet.com

CHAPTER 3: Sustainability from the Outside

ORGANIC CLOTHING

Blue Canoe: www.bluecanoe.com

Cotton Field: www.cottonfieldllc.com

Earth Wear: www.earth-wear.com

Esperanza Threads: www.esperanzathreads.com

Life Kind: www.lifekind.com

Organic Selections: www.organicselections.com

Patagonia: www.patagonia.com

Prana: www.prana.com

Sage Creek Naturals: www.sagecreeknaturals.com

Tomorrow's World: www.tomorrowsworld.com

Under the Canopy: www.underthecanopy.com

Wild Rose Farm: www.wildrosefarm.com

CHILDREN'S CLOTHING (ORGANIC)

Ecobaby: www.ecobaby.com

Kids Nature: www.kids-nature.com

DIAPERS (NATURAL AND ORGANIC)
Baby Works: www.babyworks.com
Chlorine-free/dioxin-free diapers: www.seventhgeneration.com
Ecobaby: www.ecobaby.com
gDiapers: www.gdiapers.com
Mama's Earth: www.mamasearth.com

FIRE RETARDANT-FREE CLOTHING
Earth Easy: www.eartheasy.com
Earth Speaks: www.earthspeaks.com
Safe Environment: www.safenvironment.com/children
Under the Canopy: www.underthecanopy.com

GREEN DRY CLEANING
GreenEarth Cleaning: www.greenearthcleaning.com

PERSONAL CARE PRODUCTS, INCLUDING ORGANIC COTTON TAMPONS
Eminence Organics Skin Care: www.eminenceorganics.com
Iredale Mineral Cosmetics: www.janeiredale.com
Life-Flo: www.life-flo.com
Natracare: www.natracare.com
Organic Essentials: www.organicessentials.com
Seventh Generation: www.seventhgeneration.com

SKIN AND BODY CARE (NATURAL AND ORGANIC)
Aubrey Organics: www.aubrey-organics.com
Avalon Organics: www.avalonorganics.com
Aveda: www.aveda.com
Jason Natural: www.jason-natural.com
Kiss My Face: www.kissmyface.com
MyChelle Dermaceuticals: www.mychelleusa.com

SAFER SUNSCREENS
Aubrey Organics: www.aubrey-organics.com

COSMETICS (NATURAL AND ORGANIC)
Afterglow Cosmetics: www.afterglowcostmerics.com
Eccobella: www.eccobella.com
Peacekeeper Cosmetics: www.iamapeacekeeper.com

TOOTHPASTE
Jason Natural: www.jason-natural.com
Tom's of Maine: www.tomsofmaine.com

For air and water filters, see Chapter 2 resources.

CHAPTER 4: Sustainability in the Home
CLEANING SUPPLIES
Bi-O-Kleen: www.bi-o-kleen.com
Earth 911: www.earth911.org
Orange TKO: www.tkoorange.com
PerfectClean Ultramicrofiber Mops, Wipes, & Dusters: www.SixWise.com
Seventh Generation: www.seventhgeneration.com

RECIPES FOR GREEN CLEANING PRODUCTS
AVAILABLE AT THESE WEBSITES:
http://www.almanacnews.com/morgue/2004/2004_05_12.clean.shtml
http://www.circleoflifefoundation.org/education/sustainable/greening/
    green_cleaning.pdf

AIR PURIFIERS
N.E.E.D.S.: www.needs.com
Nirvana Safe Haven: www.nontoxic.com

WATER PURIFIERS
New Wave Enviro Products: www.newwaveenviro.com

PAPER PRODUCTS
Seventh Generation: www.seventhgeneration.com

CORN PLASTIC PRODUCTS
Nature Works: www.natureworks.com

ORGANIC MATTRESSES/BEDDING
A Happy Planet: www.ahappyplanet.com
Daliya's Robison's website: www.nontoxic.com
EcoBedroom: www.ecobedroom.com
Heart of Vermont: www.heartofvermont.com
Holy Lamb Organics: www.holylamborganics
Lifekind: www.lifekind.com
Loop Organic: www.looporganic.com
Natura Bed Systems: www.nontoxic.com/natura
Natural Spaces: www.naturalspaces.com
Pure Rest: www.purerest.com.
Sage Creek Naturals: www.sagecreeknaturals.com
Tempur-Pedic: www.tempurpedic.com

HARDWOOD FURNITURE
A Happy Planet: www.ahappyplanet.com
Eco-furniture: www.eco-furniture.com

LAWN AND GARDEN PRODUCTS (NATURAL AND ORGANIC)
Gardens Alive: www.gardensalive.com

CHAPTER 5: Sustainable Building and Retrofitting
ARCHITECTS AND DESIGNERS
Bob Swain: www.bobswain.com
Green Business Network: www.greenerbuildings.com

GENERAL BUILDING INFORMATION
Sustainable Sources: www.greenbuilder.com

ENVIRONMENTAL TESTING SERVICES

Accutest Laboratories: www.accutest.com
AnaCon Laboratories: www.anaconlab.com
GE: www.ionics.com
GeoLabs, Inc.: www.geolabs.com
Horiba: www.horiba.com

NON-OFFGASSING BUILDING MATERIALS

Green Building Resource Guide: www.greenguide.com
Shasta Energy Group: www.shastaenergygroup.org

NATURAL CARPETS

EcoChoices: www.ecobydesign.com
Nirvana Safe Haven: www.nontoxic.com

RENEWABLE ENERGY

Gaiam: www.realgoods.com
Global Resource Options: www.globalresourceoptions.com
Mayflower Trading Company: www.mayflowertrading.com
REC Solar: www.ecoenergies.com
Also see: www.solarenergy.com

NATURAL LIGHT

EcoChoices: www.ecobydesign.com
Nirvana Safe Haven: www.nontoxic.com

NON-OFFGASSING PAINTS

AURO: www.aurousa.com
BioShieldPaint: www.bioshieldpaint.com
Crystal Air: www.nontoxic.com
Old Fashioned Milk Paint Company: www.milkpaint.com
Oshadhi USA: www.oshadhiusa.com
Sawyer Finn Natural Milk Paints: www.sawyerfinn.com
Weather-Bos: www.weatherbos.com

SUSTAINABLE BUILDING MATERIALS

Building For Health Materials Center: www.buildingforhealth.com

EcoBusinessLinks:www.ecobusinesslinks.com/links/
   sustainable_building_supplies.htm

Icynene: www.icynene.com

ALTERNATIVE ENERGY SOURCES

3 Phases: www.3phases.com

Forcefield: www.otherpower.com

Gaiam: www.realgoods.com

Renewable Choice Energy: www.renewablechoice.com

TerraPass: www.terrapass.com

Also see: www.carbonfund.org

PROGRAMMABLE THERMOSTATS

Look for the Energy Star label, which can be found on home appliances
everywhere—home supply stores, Sears, etc.

SICK BUILDING SYNDROME

WellBuilding: www.wellbuilding.com

CHAPTER 6: Energy Sustainability: Time for Renewal

GENERAL RESOURCES ON RENEWABLE ENERGY

Ecology Center: www.ecocenter.org

Environmental News Network:
   www.enn.com/alternative_energy_d.html

Health Goods: www.healthgoods.com

Home Power magazine: www.homepower.com

Real Goods: www.realgoods.com

Renewable Choice: www.renewablechoice.com

U.S. Department of Energy's division of Energy Efficiency and
   Renewable Energy (includes information about renewable energy
   and alternative fuel vehicles): www.eere.energy.gov

GLOBAL WARMING

EPA: www.epa.gov/globalwarming
Sierra Club: www.sierraclub.org/globalwarming
Also see: www.worldviewofglobalwarming.com

HYBRIDS AND FUEL

EPA: www.fueleconomy.gov
Green Car Club: www.nesea.org/greencarclub
National Biodiesel Board: www.biodiesel.org
NEVC: www.e85fuel.com
TerraPass: www.terrapass.com
Toyota: www.toyotausa.com

SOLAR CELL PHONE CHARGER

REI: www.rei.com

SOLAR POWER

American Solar Energy Society: www.ases.org
Find Solar: www.findsolar.com
Solar Electric Light Fund (SELF): www.self.org

WIND POWER

3 Phases: www.3phases.com
American Wind Energy Association:
    http://www.awea.org/faq/rsdntqa.html#cost
Residential wind turbines: http://www.cetsolar.com/windgen.htm

CARBON FOOTPRINT CALCULATORS

Carbonfund: www.carbonfund.org
SafeClimate: www.safeclimate.net/calculator/

CHAPTER 7: A Sustainable Future

SUSTAINABLE BUSINESS

Global Reporting Initiative: www.globalreporting.org

SUSTAINABLE COMMUNITIES

EnviroLink: www.envirolink.org

Monterey Bay Aquarium: www.mbayaq.org

GREEN TECHNOLOGIES

ENV: www.envbike.com

References

CHAPTER 1: A New Way of Life

Edwards, Andres, *The Sustainability Revolution* (New Society Publishers, 2005).

CHAPTER 2: Sustainability from the Inside

Appleton, Nancy, *Lick the Sugar Habit* (Avery, 1996).

Batmanghelidj, F., *Water for Health, for Healing, for Life: You're Not Sick, You're Thirsty!* (Warner Books, 2003).

Chilton, Ski, *Inflammation Nation* (Fireside, 2004).

Dufty, William, *Sugar Blues* (Warner Books, re-issued 1986).

WEBSITES

www.wellbuilding.com

BANANA AGRICULTURE

Pesticide News website: http://www.pan-uk.org/pestnews/ pn48/pn48p9.htm

CHEMICAL TOXICITY

Walter J. Crinnion, N.D., from a chapter in *Organic Gardening Almanac* (Llewellyn, 1995).

PHTHALATE TOXICITY

Comprehensive info available at: http://www.ithyroid.com/phthalates.htm

Blount, B.C., Silva, M.J., et al. "Levels of seven urinary phthalate metabolites in a human reference population." *Environmental Health Perspectives*, 2000 Oct;108(10):979-82.

Centers for Disease Control and Prevention, Report, July 2005, available at: http://www.cdc.gov/exposurereport/pdf/factsheet_phthalates.pdf

Colborn, Theo, Dumanoski, Dianne, Myers, John Peterson, *Our Stolen Future* (Plume Books, 1997).

Colón, I., Caro, D., et al. "Identification of phthalate esters in the serum of young Puerto Rican girls with premature breast development." *Environmental Health Perspectives*, 2000;108(9):895-900.

Herman-Giddens, M.E., Slora, E.J., et al. "Secondary sexual characteristics and menses in young girls seen in office practice: a study from the pediatric research in office settings network." *Pediatrics*, 1997;99(4):505-512.

SUGAR TOXICITY

Appleton, Nancy, *Lick the Sugar Habit* (Avery, 1996).

Bernstein, J., et al. "Depression of lymphocyte transformation following oral glucose ingestion." *American Journal of Clinical Nutrition*, 1997;30:613.

Couzy, F., et al. "Nutritional implications of the interaction minerals." *Progressive Food and Nutrition Science*, 1993;17(1):65-87.

Darlington, L., Ramsey, N.W. & Mansfield, J. R. "Placebo controlled, blind study of dietary manipulation therapy in rheumatoid arthritis." *Lancet*, Feb 1986;8475(1):236-8.

Kelsay, J., et al. "Diets high in glucose or sucrose and young women." *American Journal of Clinical Nutrition*, 1974;27:926-936.

Lee, A. T. & Cerami, A. "The role of glycation in aging." *Annals of the New York Academy of Science*, 1992;663:63-67.

Mohanty P., et al. "Glucose challenge stimulates reactive oxygen species (ROS) generation by leucocytes." *Journal of Clinical Endocrinology and Metabolism*, Aug 2000; 85(8):2970-3.

Ringsdorf, W., Cheraskin, E. and Ramsay R. "Sucrose, neutrophilic phagocytosis and resistance to disease." *Dental Survey*, 1976;52(12):46-8.

Sanchez, A., et al. "Role of sugars in human neutrophilic phagocytosis." American *Journal of Clinical Nutrition*, Nov 1973;261:1180-4.

Scanto, S. & Yudkin, J. "The effect of dietary sucrose on blood lipids, serum insulin, platelet adhesiveness and body weight in human volunteers." *Postgraduate Medicine Journal*, 1969;45:602-7.

Thomas, B. J., et al. "Relation of habitual diet to fasting plasma insulin concentration and the insulin response to oral glucose." *Human Nutrition Clinical Nutrition*, 1983;36C(1):49-51.

Tominaga, M., et al. "Impaired glucose tolerance is a risk factor for cardiovascular disease, but not fasting glucose." *Diabetes Care*, 1999:2(6):920-4.

Tragnone, A. et al. "Dietary habits as risk factors for inflammatory bowel disease." *Eur J Gastroenterol Hepatol*, Jan 1995;7(1):47-51.

Vaccaro O., Ruth, K. J. & Stamler J. "Relationship of postload plasma glucose to mortality with 19 year follow-up." *Diabetes Care*, Oct 15,1992;10:328-34.

FLUORIDE TOXICITY

Magaziner, Allen, Bonvie, Linda & Zolezzi, Anthony *Chemical-Free Kids* (Twin Streams/Kensington, 2003) pp. 20-21.

BEEF PRODUCTION

From an article originally published in *Canada EarthSaver*, April/May 1997, available at: http://www.earthsave.bc.ca/materials/articles/articles/pdf/enviro/ why_does_the_earth.pdf

BOTTLED WATER

From an article by Emily Arnold and Janet Larsen, published by Earth Policy Institute, February 2006, available at: http://www.earth-policy.org/Updates/2006/Update51.htm

PLASTIC AND NALGENE WATER BOTTLES
Doheny, B. "Nalgene plastic may be harmful." *Daily Barometer Online*, available at: http://barometer.orst.edu/vnews/display.v/ART/2004/02/ 17/40324e5d40a14?in_archive=1
"Nalgene water bottles appear to be unsafe." Available at: http://www.mercola.com/2004/apr/7/nalgene_water.htm

CHEMICALS IN POTATO CHIPS
"Acrylamide and Proposition 65." California OEHHA website, May 2005, available at: www.oehha.ca.gov/prop65/acrylamideqa.html

CHAPTER 3: Sustainability from the Outside
Harte, John, Holdren, Cheryl, et al., *Toxics A to Z* (University of California Press, 1991).
Magaziner, Allan, *Chemical-Free Kids* (Twin Streams, Kensington, 2003).
Steinman, David, *Living Healthy in Toxic World* (Berkley, 1996).
Winter, Ruth, *A Consumer Dictionary of Cosmetic Ingredients* (Three River Press, 2005).

WEBSITES
Marci Zaroff's website, www.underthecanopy.com, contains a large amount of reference materials on this subject.
Good site for risks of various clothing, personal care and food products: http://www.ecologycenter.org/erc/petroleum/body.html
www.patagonia.com
Listing of cosmetics and their toxic contents: http://www.ewg.org/reports/skindeep/
Good resource site for risks associated with clothing, cosmetics and body care products: http://www.ecologycenter.org/erc/petroleum/body.html

HAIR DYE
Kirkland, D.J., Henderson, L, et al. "Testing strategies in mutagenicity and genetic toxicology: an appraisal of the guidelines of the European Scientific Committee for Cosmetics and Non-Food Products for the evaluation of hair dyes." *Mutation Research*, 2005 Dec 30;588(2):88-105. Epub 2005 Dec 2.
Marzulli, F.N., Watlington, P.M., et al. "Exploratory skin penetration findings relating to the use of lead acetate hair dyes. Hair as a test tissue for monitoring uptake of systemic lead." *Current Problems in Dermatology*, 1978;7:196-204.
Xavier University study on lead in hair dye was reported by CNN on Feb. 2, 1997 and published in *Journal of American Pharmaceutical Association*.

SUNSCREENS
Heneweer, M., Muusse, M., et al. "Additive estrogenic effects of mixtures of frequently used UV filters on pS2-gene transcription in MCF-7 cells." *Toxicology and Applied Pharmacology*, 2005 Oct 15;208(2):170-7.

Sarveiya, V., Risk, S., et al. "Liquid chromatographic assay for common sunscreen agents: application to in vivo assessment of skin penetration and systemic absorption in human volunteers." *J Chromatograhy B Analyt Technol Biomed Life Sci*, 2004 Apr 25;803(2);225-31.

CHLORINE
Interestingly, the article in which the government warned of the cancer and cardiovascular disease risks associated with chlorine are widely reported on the Internet, but the text of the original article published by the White House's Council of Environmental Quality on July 31, 2003, is not available.

PHTHLATES
Blount, B.C., Silva, M.J., et al. "Levels of seven urinary phthalate metabolites in a human reference population." *Environmental Health Perspectives*, 2000 Oct;108(10):979-82.

PESTICIDE RESIDUES
Bronaugh, R.L., Stewart, R.F., et al. "Extent of cutaneous metabolism during percutaneous absorption of xenobiotics." *Toxicology and Applied Pharmacology*, 1989 Jul;99(3);534-43.

TOXINS IN CORD BLOOD
Brant, M. "Toxic waste." *Newsweek*, Newsweek Web Exclusive, July 27, 2005, www.newsweek.com.

ALUMINUM-BASED ANTIPERSPIRANTS
Darbre, P.D. "Metalloestrogens: An emerging class of inorganic xenoestrogens with potential to add to the oestrogenic burden of the human breast." *Journal of Applied Toxicology*, 2006 May-Jun;26(3):191-7.

CHAPTER 4: Sustainability in the Home
Berthold-Bond, Annie, *Clean Green* (Ceres Press, 1994).
Dadd, Debra Lynn, *Home Safe Home* (Archer/Penguin, 2004).
Wolverton, B.C., *How to Grow Fresh Air* (Penguin, 1998).

ENERGY CONSUMPTION STATISTICS
Energy Information Administration website: http://www.eia.doe.gov/kids/ classactivities/CrunchTheNumbersIntermediateDec2002.pdf
USGS website: http://energy.cr.usgs.gov/energy/stats_ctry/Stat1.htmla

SAVING WITH RECYCLING
NRDC website: http://www.nrdc.org/land/forests/gtissue.asp

SAVING WITH COMPACT FLUORESCENTS
Environmental Defense website: http://www.environmentaldefense.org/ article.cfm?contentid=5215

SAVING WITH RECYCLING

NDRC website: http://www.nrdc.org/land/forests/gtissue.asp

LAWN CARE AND FERTILIZER USE

www.greens.org

CLEANING CHEMICALS

www.restoreproducts.com

PESTICIDES

Cook, C. "The spraying of America." *Earth Island Journal*, Spring 2005, available at: http://www.thirdworldtraveler.com/Environment/Spraying_America.html

Lowengart, R.A., Peters, J.M., et al. "Childhood leukemia and parents' occupational and home exposures." *Journal of the National Cancer Institute*, 1987;79:39-46. National Cancer Institute, study on pesticides and cancer.

FERTILIZER AND OIL

Pfeiffer, D.A. "Eating fossil fuels." From The Wilderness Publications, 2004, available at: www.fromthewilderness.com/free/ww3/100303_eating_oil.html

CHAPTER 5: Sustainable Building and Retrofitting

WEBSITES

Bob Swain's website: www.bobswain.com

General building information: www.greenbuilder.com

Alternative energy systems, products and installation: www.utilityfree.com

SALINE POOL SYSTEMS

www.salinepoolsystems.com

CONSTRUCTION STATISTICS

Roodman, M. & Lenssen, N. *A Building Revolution: How Ecology and Health Concerns Are Transforming Construction*, Worldwatch Paper 124, Worldwatch Institute, Washington, D.C., March 1995.

SICK BUILDING SYNDROME

www.welllbuilding.com

CHAPTER 6: Energy Sustainability: Time for Renewal

RENEWABLE RESOURCES

www.green-e.org

www.greenfacts.org

www.greentagsusa.org

ENERGY CONSUMPTION FIGURES

www.sustainabletable.org

ELECTRIC CONSUMPTION
Healthgoods website: http://www.healthgoods.com/Shopping/Conservation_Products/
Conservation_Products.htm

ALTERNATIVE VEHICLES AND FUELS
www.eere.energy.gov

CAR MILEAGE
Environmental Defense website: http://www.environmentaldefense.org/
article.cfm?contentid=5215

WIND ENERGY
American Wind Energy Association:
http://www.awea.org/pubs/factsheets/WindPowerTodayFinal.pdf

CARBON FOOTPRINT CALCULATORS
www.carbonfund.org   www.safeclimate.net/calculator/

CHAPTER 7: The Big Picture
SUSTAINABLE BUSINESS
Global Reporting Initiative: www.globalreporting.org

SUSTAINABLE COMMUNITIES
www.envirolink.org

COFFEE PRICES PROCEEDS TO GROWER
Instituto Observatório Social website: www.observatoriosocial.org.br/download/cafeing.pdf

AMAZON SPECIES
PBS website: www.pbs.org/journeyintoamazonia/about.html

LARGE FISH DECLINE 90% OVER PAST 50 YEARS
Larsen, J. "Wild fish catch hits limits." Earth Policy Institute website, 2005, available at:
www.earth-policy.org/Indicators/Fish/2005.htm

WIND POWER INSTALLED BASE
www.answers.com

Index

NOTES

NOTES

NOTES

NOTES

NOTES